Prayers from the Mount

Also by J. Barrie Shepherd

Diary of Daily Prayer

*A Diary of Prayer: Daily Meditations
on the Parables of Jesus*

*Encounters: Poetic Meditations
on the Old Testament*

Prayers
from the
Mount

J. Barrie Shepherd

The Westminster Press
Philadelphia

Book design by Gene Harris

First edition

Published by The Westminster Press®
Philadelphia, Pennsylvania

PRINTED IN THE UNITED STATES OF AMERICA
9 8 7 6 5 4 3 2 1

Library of Congress Cataloging-in-Publication Data

Shepherd, J. Barrie.
  Prayers from the mount.

  1. Sermon on the mount—Meditations.   2. Bible.
N.T.   Matthew V–VII—Meditations.   3. Prayers.
I. Title.
BT380.2.S45   1986   242'.5   85-26400
ISBN 0-664-24699-0 (pbk.)

Contents

I dedicate this book in gratitude
to the people of Chebeague Island, Maine,
whose acceptance, friendship, and encouragement
of a mere "summer person/parson" gave me
the setting and, at times, the inspiration
to complete this and my other writings.

Preface

The prayer diary is a form which I—and several other authors—have borrowed from the late John Baillie. Baillie's classic, *A Diary of Private Prayer,* published nearly forty years ago, showed the way for a whole generation and more to set their own experience of daily prayer within a disciplined yet personal and adaptable structure.

In this current volume, the diary format of daily morning and evening prayers has been maintained. For reasons of size and economy, however, it proved impractical to provide a full blank page for diary purposes—the making of notes, the composing of one's own prayers and poetry—as was done in my previous two such books. At least some space is available between the prayers, and I would encourage the reader/prayer to use this feature fully; to make this book your own; to create in it and of it your personal journal of "Prayers from the Mount."

The scripture readings listed at the start of every day should be read in full before praying the prayers for that day. In many cases I have only given a brief segment of the chosen portion. Please take the time to read and meditate upon the entire passage on which the prayers are based. I would also recommend that daily readings from a lectionary or other such guide be included in order to fill out these somewhat narrow selections with the fullness of the Word.

Many of these prayers will seem quite personal in places. They reflect my own experience of the Lord, and of his presence in my life, and therefore cannot fully also be the reader's. I make no apology for this. Prayers like these need to be personal. Indeed,

I have often found that the more particular and personal one can be, the more universal is one's appeal. Such passages have often proved to be the ones that have evoked the warmest, most grateful responses in the past.

Finally, a word about language. As the father of four daughters, former chaplain and professor at what was then Connecticut College for Women, I count myself as reasonably well sensitized to the questions of male and female terminology. Since well before my first book—eleven years ago now—I have made a practice of avoiding all generic male terms in speaking of members of the human race. However, in addressing God, I still find myself committed to that familial word, "Father." Yes, I can and have addressed God as "Mother," just to prove the point. But "Father" is the name that I grew up with, the name that Jesus taught, and, on a point of personal privilege, I have used it in my book. To any and all who are disturbed by this I offer my sincere apologies and the hope that, even so, this book may be for them a source of blessing.

DAY ONE
The Gathering
Matthew 5:1–2

Seeing the crowds, he went up on the mountain, and when he sat down his disciples came to him. And he opened his mouth and taught them.

MORNING

Lord Jesus, when I think of this Sermon on the Mount
I imagine you raised up a little, on a green and sloping hillside,
perhaps atop a rocky outcrop or a grassy knoll, and surrounded
by a vast, attentive throng.
Yet when I read the verses here in Matthew
it doesn't seem like that at all, seems as if you went
up on the mountain to avoid the crowds and have some time
alone with your newly called disciples.

Is there, then, a sense in which these teachings
were not intended for the masses, not meant to be a vague
and general Golden Rule, a well-repeated-hardly-ever-studied
set of guidelines for successful living
that everyone can swear by?
Might it be that in these sayings you set out,
in fact, to train your inner circle, to prepare the leaders,
shape the leaven for the loaf? These are no vague,
innocuous remarks; no general, all-purpose code
to suit all situations. These are demanding,
even frightening, words. They call us to do things,
be things, that we would rather leave to someone else.

Help me, in the days ahead, Lord Jesus,
to clean away the smear and smudge of long familiarity
and hear your sayings fresh and newly minted;

11

thus to know your call anew, its blessings,
its demands, and then to follow where they lead me
on the pilgrim path that you have walked before.

Amen.

EVENING

You went into the hills, Lord,
withdrew, it seems, from all the crowds,
and spoke these timeless teachings to your chosen followers,
just as they speak to all of us, the ones you call
to service and to sacrifice today.

I wonder how they received your word.
Did they complain, perhaps, murmur that you
asked of them too much, that no one living could fulfill
these sayings, could meet all the stiff requirements
of your kingdom? Did they, maybe, draw up,
in private, their own counter propositions and then demand
that both of them be sent to arbitration?
I have a hunch that's how folk might react to you today.
I have a fear that I too might respond in such a way.

Yet your disciples saw these words, not as prescription
but as privilege, not as a duty but as a delight!
They greeted them with joy, we can be sure,
rejoicing to be counted worthy of such a challenge.

Why do we still reject the way of life, Lord?
Or, at best, accept it grudgingly as a dreadful,
heavy burden to be borne? Show me, this night,
the radiant glory of your teachings and your precepts.

Let them shine out from the holy page into my
all-too-unholy mind, my heart, my daily walk.

So bring to me again, O Lord,
the joy of thy salvation. And let my spirit
sing before I sleep, renew itself in you during
the darkened hours, and arise to rediscover
the abundance of new life.
Amen.

DAY TWO
The Blessed Poor
Matthew 5:3

Blessed are the poor in spirit, for theirs is the kingdom of heaven.

MORNING

This saying of yours has been misused, Lord Jesus.
Those who are not poor have taken it to mean that it's all right
for others to know poverty, that human deprivation is
an unavoidable reality, part of "the way things are";
even that the poor are somehow luckier than they:
they do not have the complications, worries, and responsibilities,
the great decisions, burdens, that the affluent have to bear.

Such self-justifying nonsense
could never have crossed your lips, Lord,
for you knew, yourself, the crushing weight of poverty,
grew up within the household of a simple country carpenter.
You fed the famished, healed the hopeless,
welcomed to your side those without refuge.
Your daily walk led you among the wretched of the earth,
the beggars, whores, and outcasts, those who bear
the bitter fate of cruel misfortune or their own foolish mistakes.
You knew that there is nothing at all "blessed" in the kind
of desperation that we witness in our cities, that we learn of,
every day, in the news from the Third World.

Help me this day, as I confront the poor,
whether in individual lives or in the issues, policies,
ethical decisions of our times, help me to see them as you
always knew them . . . brothers, sisters, fellow members

of God's family. Then encourage me to spend my time, my gifts,
my self in such ways as even yet may prove
a blessing to at least one other
human being who is less
well off than I.
                    Amen.

EVENING

When the disciples heard these words
they could have been forgiven an ironic smile.
For they had given up all they had, left everything behind—
boats, nets, homes, even wives and children—and might well
have been wondering just what it was lay up ahead.
"Of no fixed abode" was just as true of them as of any
old bag lady or vent man in the city of today.

Yet you called them "blessed," Lord . . .
blessed because, in giving up the things they thought they owned,
they were beginning to discover their true birthright,
one that they could never lose . . . blessed because, in making
themselves totally dependent on your Father in heaven, they had
become totally independent of anything else in all creation . . .
blessed because your kind of poverty is so much richer than
the wealth of those who have only money to support them . . .
blessed finally because, in pouring themselves out,
they will share in the self-giving of our God
who is most fully himself in such self-giving.

Lead me, Lord, in the paths of such a poverty.
Teach me not to be possessed by my possessions, controlled
by my lust to control and own. Show me how to hold this world
and all its gifts in stewardship, not ownership.

Let me be defined, not by what I have,
but by who I am and whose I am.
Then claim me for your own.

                    Amen.

DAY THREE
The Sorrowful
Matthew 5:4

Blessed are those who mourn, for they shall be comforted.

MORNING

It doesn't make sense, Lord,
"Blessed are those who mourn." You might as well say,
"Full are the hungry," "Healthy are the sick," even, "Alive
are the dead." It is a contradiction in terms—
"Happy are the sad."
How can anyone make sense of it?

One thing: at least this word of yours
speaks to the world we live in. For sadness, mourning,
is a real and important part of our experience. We mourn
the loss of innocence, of youthful dedication, of ideals, goals,
long lost within our daily lives. We grieve about the daily
tragedies, the fires and crashes, bombings, the starvation,
and the slaughter that deface each morning's headlines.
We weep for those within our closer circle who face death,
or have already passed beyond. When you said,
"Those who mourn," Lord Jesus,
you spoke to every one of us, you speak
to me this morning as I pray this prayer.

True mourning, after all, is an experience of love.
If we did not love we would not grieve, and there have been
those who would protect themselves from all such loss
by never loving anyone. Poor souls!

Help me, this day, to recognize the sadness
of our world, the *lachrymae rerum,* the basic tears within
all things that are essential to the fullest knowing of this
human life in all its height and depth. Then lead me
toward blessing in my tears, Lord. Reveal to me the love
that lies right at the core of grief, and from that love teach me
to grow, yes, show me how to turn my tears, the grief of others,
into sure and steady laughter through the wonder of
this word of yours, "Blessed are those who mourn."

Amen.

EVENING

"They shall be comforted . . . "
Comfort, Lord, can be something of a mixed blessing;
mixed, in that most of us would rather not require it
in the first place. It conjures for us images of childhood,
of a mother's soothing embrace after falling from
a bicycle, or failing in some test of strength or skill.
It brings an almost physical sensation of warm acceptance,
soft and gentle tenderness, a complete easing
of all stress and pain.

Yet this word "comfort" has a further meaning.
Its Latin root, *con fortis,* means "with strength."
Thus, to be comforted by you can mean
not just to be appeased
but to be joined, to be accompanied by One who brings
not ease or self-indulgent pity but, rather, reinforcements.
Comfort, in this understanding, is made up of courage,
fortitude, and faith; is the gift of strength sufficient
to renew the struggle, reenter the race, take up,

18

again, the building of your kingdom, Lord,
that kingdom yet to be of justice, family, and peace.

So, as I sleep this night,
renew my strength from yours, my Savior.
That, resting in your comfort, I might rise refreshed
to set forth once again upon the way of service,
upon the royal way of love.

Amen.

DAY FOUR

The Meek

Matthew 5:5

Blessed are the meek, for they shall inherit the earth.

MORNING

Born losers, that's what we think of the Meek,
Lord, spineless jellyfish, who daren't say "Boo!"
to their own shadow. And as for inheriting anything,
let alone the earth—what a laugh! It takes power
to inherit nowadays: power, influence, clout. The Meek
couldn't even punch their way out of a paper bag.
You certainly had a rich sense of humor when you said,
"Blessed are the meek. . . ."

On the other hand, Lord, you didn't just bless
the Meek, you joined them. "Take my yoke upon you,
and learn of me; for I am meek and lowly in heart."
You said it of yourself more than once.
And although you were meek, there was certainly
nothing of the doormat about you.
As you tramped the hills of Galilee, rebuked the stormy seas,
fed and healed the multitudes, tangled mind and wit
with wily scribes and Pharisees, and cast the money changers
from the temple, you showed us that, whatever meekness is,
it is not cowardice, or lack of backbone or moral fiber.

Meekness seems to be all caught up in how
we think about ourselves, Lord Jesus. Not that we
have to think we're terrible, reject ourselves, condemn
our every thought and deed; more that we can stop worrying

20

about ourselves. We can see ourselves as you did,
not the all-devouring obsession of our every waking hour,
but the self as gift of God, a gift to live and use in service.
Meekness means the self in its true place. Not in the center.
God lays claim to that. Self, rather, at the limits,
on the boundary where life encounters life,
and needs and fears and even hates
are met and neutralized by love.

Jesus, shape my meekness. Let it be
a thing of daring, style, and selfless grace,
a walking in your footsteps, Lord.
                                        Amen.

EVENING

To inherit the earth these days
you had better be tough, hard-nosed, yes, ruthless.
Excellence, after all, is what people are after,
and if you do not measure up, if the bottom line for you
is still way above your head, then you had best move over,
clear the way, and not impede the heavy traffic. Get meek,
in other words, before you get run over!

What do I really own, Lord?
What is there to inherit, when all is said and done?
Is this earth really something to be won by force of arms?
Did Hitler, Stalin, Genghis Khan, Attila, all the rest
really inherit anything beyond a six-foot plot for burial—
if that? Do not the facts of history—not dreams but facts—
suggest that if anyone has a lasting claim of gratitude,
allegiance, loyalty, even love upon the human race
it is the folk like Francis, Buddha, Gandhi,

Martin Luther King, Jr., or Mother Teresa—the gentle ones
who dreamed great dreams, then gave their lives
to live them out for all to see?

Can anyone win love, compel respect?
The one who seeks to own, seize, possess this world
will never truly inherit it, never catch or even glimpse
its loveliness. But when I walk among the trees of fall,
listen to the birds of springtime, sit quiet
in a garden in the summer sun, or crunch
the new-crisp snow of winter . . . then I inherit!
For to inherit is, above all, to receive:
to receive a gift from someone else.
It is a windfall, a surprise unearned, enjoyed.

Teach me, Lord, in the days to come,
how to receive my own inheritance. Let me seek
in this your world not to control it, own it, change it,
or subdue it; but to rejoice in it. In all I do
to glorify your holy name.
                              Amen.

DAY FIVE
The Would-Be-Goods
Matthew 5:6

Blessed are those who hunger and thirst for righteousness, for they shall be satisfied.

MORNING

People hunger and thirst for lots of things these days, Lord.
There are those who die each day for want of fundamentals—
food and drink. And then there are the rest of us,
whose hungers are daily played upon, manipulated
by the advertising world to make us want all sorts of things
that we could well, and often better, do without.

We yearn after security, planning our investments,
considering our commitments, always with an eye
to self-protection; to making sure that we are able to survive
in reasonable comfort the potential great catastrophes
of life. While all the time we know, somewhere inside,
that all such security is ultimately doomed,
for we cannot "take it with us."

Success is another goal we hunger after,
another empty dream which, even if achieved,
slips through the fingers like a handful of dry sand.
Popularity, great wealth, a life of style and elegance and power,
prestige or sexual adventure; our desires, some call them needs,
are myriad, Lord. Yes, we do hunger and thirst
after so many things.

Yet righteousness is somehow not among them, Father.
We tend to think of righteousness today as pharisaical,

confuse it with *self*-righteousness, and say, "That's not for me."
So we build our lives around such lesser goals
as achievement, or even mere survival; and then wonder
when our days seem filled with trivial pursuits, our arts
and sciences revolve around the modes of emptiness and death.

Lord, reveal to me the meaning of *your* righteousness:
your righteousness, not first as some holy, majestic, and
unapproachable essence of sheer purity;
rather, that righteousness
we saw in Jesus Christ, whose purity of love
drew men and women
to his side, whose complete integrity released such power
among us, such a cosmic magnetism, that even to this day
countless multitudes still claim him as their Savior
and their friend. Then lead me in the paths
of righteousness, this day,
and through all my days to come.

Amen.

EVENING

As I look back across this day that is now ending, Lord,
I realize that I have failed in many ways. There have been
moments, opportunities to serve and live my faith;
yet for the most part I have turned aside, chosen, instead,
to serve and live myself.

Father, my heart aches at all the high resolve
that has been disappointed. I recall the goals I set
in adolescent years: the vows of dedication in the church;
of high school or of college graduation; pledges made in marriage,
or as the parent of a newborn child; promises to you, Lord,

to myself, and other persons. Yes, I have failed to be
what I have hoped and planned and vowed to be.

Lord, can this sense of loss and grief be at least a part of what
you meant by those who "hunger and thirst for righteousness"?
Did you mean, by this, to bless that vast and yearning throng
who *would* be good, who carry on through failure and defeat,
stumbling along the way of holiness, making progress,
if at all, on hands and knees and elbows?

We *would* be better than we are, Lord.
We still would taste your more abundant life.
We cannot simply settle down to this, call all our dreams
and hopes mere youthful idealism. There is that,
set deep within, which will not let us rest content
with mediocre, self-absorbed existence.

The Hebrew sages tell us that it is your "image";
that when you first created us you formed your image at the core
to mark and guide and hold us for your own. And so,
As Augustine has said, "Our hearts are restless, Lord,
until they find their rest in thee." Whatever, Father,
I know I could do better, live more freely, give more fully;
and in my quiet moments—
as now, when I am all alone with you—
I pray that this Beatitude of yours may be fulfilled;
that my desire for wholeness, yes, and righteousness,
will one day yet be satisfied.
Amen.

DAY SIX
The Merciful
Matthew 5:7

Blessed are the merciful, for they shall obtain mercy.

MORNING

Mercy does not strike me as the kind of thing
I deal in very much, O God. I think of mercy as a quality
reserved for those in high authority. Judges can show mercy,
or generals, perhaps; monarchs, presidents,
persons of that order.
I suppose that, as a parent, I do occasionally have
the opportunity to be merciful, but in these days
of children's lib, even that is less and less the case.
No, mercy, at first glance, would seem to be beyond my sphere,
a prerogative of the mighty and the powerful.

But is this narrow, judicial view of mercy—
mercy as letting someone off from some punishment or other—
is this really what Jesus meant to talk about right here?
Is there, perhaps, a broader application, Lord,
where "mercy" can involve an attitude to all of life,
all people, not just penalties and punishments?
When Jesus told us to forgive—as he did, so many times—
he wasn't talking about bargains, deals, or any *quid pro quo*,
but rather about entire relationships, about the common ground
of grace—your forgiveness of us all—on which we stand
and meet and act toward one another.

Mercy would then become a way of life,
a gentleness and openness to others, a general disposition

to trust people, give them, at least, the benefit of the doubt.
Mercy also requires my unwillingness to condemn
any child of God,
no matter how heinous the offense may seem to me,
because the most heinous crime of all, the nailing of
your sinless Son to die upon the cross for our salvation,
called forth from him no bitter, angry word of judgment;
rather, the ultimate and surpassing word of mercy,
"Father, forgive them; for they know not what they do."

Let that mercy root itself within my life this day, Father.
May this day be permeated with your Spirit
of forgiveness.
                Amen.

EVENING

Lord, this is a merciless world and time to be alive in.
I used to think that life in other eras,
long before the great discoveries of medicine and science,
must have been brutal, short, and sharp.
Yet this twentieth-century world that I inhabit—
the gas and trenches of the First World War,
the Stalinist purges and the gulags, those millions of children
shipped to extermination in the concentration camps,
the atomic bombs, atrocities of Vietnam, Afghanistan, Iran,
South Africa, Beirut, Belfast, and now the bombs and hijackings
of terrorists—Father, this is a merciless world
and time to be alive in.

Furthermore, if I am ruthlessly honest with myself,
I must realize that I participate in this brutality.
For to the victims—those who suffer, the wounded, captives,

the bereft, the countless millions of refugees—
it matters little really whether I actually cause their pain
or just stand by and let it happen. So long as I do nothing
about suffering, I am caught up—willy-nilly—in brutality.
I am merciless, like all the rest.

Therefore, I need your mercy more than ever, Lord.
Forgive me for the ways that I have failed you,
even in this day now ending.
Have mercy on me, even though at times
I may have joined the merciless in failing to respond
to human need. Remind me, once again, and for the days
and years ahead, that—as Jesus taught—if I would truly,
fully know your mercy, then I must be merciful myself.

Thus let my life reflect your grace
in everything I do, to everyone I meet.

Amen.

DAY SEVEN
The Pure in Heart
Matthew 5:8

Blessed are the pure in heart, for they shall see God.

MORNING

This saying, Father, would seem to be reserved
for a very select group. To "see" God, after all,
to actually glimpse the beatific vision, is something
even the saints, or most of them, have sought after in vain.

That tale of Moses in the book of Exodus has long intrigued me,
Father, when he begged to see your glory. You set him in a cleft
on Sinai and then "passed by." Yet even Moses glimpsed only
your back; for the vision of your face could not be seen
except the seer forfeit life in the encounter.

I recall the great Aquinas, scholar-monk and father-in-theology
of much of Catholic doctrine, who, late in life, experienced
the vision of your presence and thereafter vowed that all
that he had written, the unsurpassed creation of his mind and pen,
was as mere worthless straw compared to what
he had been privileged to see.
"They shall see God": that is a promise, a reward, Father,
seldom attained, at least in this life.

There have been moments, all the same,
and still are, now and then, when, if not a direct vision,
still the sureness of your presence breaks in upon me,
drives me to my knees at my unworthiness,
fills my eyes with tears

of mixed regret and joy and love that, despite everything I have
done and not done, you would touch my life again and use it,
somehow claim it for your own.
There are times I am transfixed by the sheer splendor
of your vast and intricate creation; instants when the realm
of human creativity, in art and literature and music, lifts me
to the heights of self-forgetfulness and self-surrender.
And once or twice in prayer, Lord God,
your Son has stood so close, his quiet reassuring presence
just behind, his hand above my shoulder, almost touching
my bowed head, that I have brushed the fringes of that bliss
that cannot be described, only received in wonder.

In the power of such moments,
in the promise they hold out, I now begin this day.

Amen.

EVENING

Purity in anything seems difficult to find
in this mixed and mixed-up world, Father.
I call to mind a building of pure loveliness and grace
that I saw some years ago as I stood upon the very spot where
Jesus said these words, the Mount of the Beatitudes in Galilee.
It was a little chapel set into the hillside:
a simple place of clean, uncluttered elegance, immaculate,
and filled with radiant light.
Yet that place of pure unblemished beauty was built
by order of Il Duce, Mussolini—Fascist dictator of Italy.
Yes, purity, in this corrupt and polluted world, this world where
even elemental water, air, and soil have lost their innocence,
purity is an endangered thing.

Even within the soul, Lord, the spirit-psyche with all
its tangled motivations, the ego, superego, and the id,
the unconscious and subconscious realms
of being and experience,
even within the soul itself it is difficult to recognize
this purity of heart.

Yet if I look at Jesus as I find him in the Gospels,
I find no stained-glass saint; no squeaky-clean, untouchable,
unapproachably perfect paragon of every virtue. Instead I find
a purity of love, an unconditional, uncompromising openness
to human need and pain and trembling hope; a commitment there,
no matter what, to give himself in every way conceivable
to win us for your grace, to call us back into
your family, your household.

Even so, as I meet those who are in need,
in suffering or in fear let my heart be pure,
cleansed of every selfish, faithless impulse, pure
in love to see you, recognize, and then respond to your clear call
wherever you may meet me in the lonely, lost, and weary
of this world.
                    Amen.

DAY EIGHT
The Peacemakers
Matthew 5:9

Blessed are the peacemakers, for they shall be called children of God.

MORNING

Peacemaking is such a nice, positive expression, Lord.
It seems like something no one could oppose or get upset about.
We hear about it, sing and pray about it in our church. But when
we start to think about it, that's when troubles start.
It's ironic, really, that perhaps the quickest, surest way
to spark dispute is to talk or preach or teach there about peace.

There are all those dreadful facts to be faced, Father,
grim statistics spread across the balance sheet of terror,
thousands, tens of thousands of nuclear devices,
each one many times more powerful than
the Hiroshima holocaust, each one targeted
on me or folk just like me, more or less,
in houses, churches, towns and cities
all across this globe.

It's not easy, Lord, not easy to visualize yourself
or, even worse, your spouse, parents, children incinerated
in the twinkling of an eye; or, yet more terrible,
struggling to die a cruel, lingering death
among the few unfortunate survivors.
It's too difficult, too depressing to think like this, to face
these horrifying facts of modern life, and so we shut them out.
We say, "What can I do? What can one person do?"
while we listen

32

to that high, persistent whine on the car radio, the calm,
collected voice of the announcer reassuring us that this is
"only a test." Yet somewhere in a corner of the brain,
another still small voice persists, "What if it were not?
What if this were really it? Would he still sound so calm?
Would she have any more to tell us than she has right now?"

Lord, I am afraid to get involved in peacemaking.
It would set people against me; set my mind, my life in turmoil,
freeze my heart in icy fear. I prefer simply to hope
that whatever happens waits until I'm dead and gone
and out of it.

Arouse me from this foolishness, Lord God.
Show me the shamefulness, the cowardice that would settle
for a future world populated—as the scientists assert—
by cockroaches, if only I can live my given span in cozy
if uneasy ignorance. And set me to the building up of peace,
step by step, day by day, and person by person; that individuals
all across your creation might work and pray and act for peace
in every way conceivable. And let me begin today, Father.
Let me begin today.
                    Amen.

EVENING

There is something in this human nature, Lord,
that makes it appear riskier to trust than to mistrust.
So in this matter of World Peace we, your people, have relied
upon the concept of M.A.D.—Mutually Assured Destruction—
whereby whoever would attack must be assured
that the other side, though devastated,
can still wreak total havoc.
We crouch behind defensive walls, walls that grow even higher
in an insane arms race; although the higher that walls are built,
the more likely they will topple; although some glitch on
a computer, some meteor shower, some fanatic with a finger
on the button could tip the deadly balance, begin
the end of everything.

The other option, Father, the other risk you offer,
is that of trusting just a bit, of believing that no nation,
no government—however different in history or experience
from ours—will deliberately destroy all life
on our planet. Why do we find it easier, Lord, to risk
everything in war than to take measured risks for peace?
Why do we still murmur, "Better dead than Red,"
when "dead" means not just me
but every "me" that ever lived or ever will;
when "Red" today can signify a gamut of political arrangements
from the terror of Stalin's Russia to the signs of hope,
diversity, and evolution emerging in such lands
as China, Hungary, Rumania, Yugoslavia?

Lord, you are the Creator both of atomic science
and of the human beings who abuse it. Grant to your people
courage to face up to the terrifying issues of our time. Grant us
the wisdom to choose ways of action that will not cause further
division, but open up new doors for trust. Give us strength
never to weary in this most important challenge of our lives.
And give us faith that, despite the looming horror, our times are
in your hands; and that through us and beyond us you are at work
to bring about your kingdom of true peace,
in Jesus Christ, the Prince of Peace.
                                        Amen.

DAY NINE
The Persecuted
Matthew 5:10

Blessed are those who are persecuted for righteousness' sake, for theirs is the kingdom of heaven.

MORNING

You made no secret of it, Lord Jesus,
that persecution was the path your followers must tread.
Repeatedly you told them all in clear explicit terms that a cross
lay at the end of your journey and of theirs; that life must
be given up, be lost, in order to be found; that trials
and imprisonment, floggings, death were part and parcel
of the pilgrimage you called them to. You painted
no false pictures, issued no deceptive invitations, Lord.

The miracle is—and perhaps this should be seen as
one of the greatest of them all—the miracle is that they
responded anyway. What an attraction,
Lord, you must have held
that, despite your constant warnings of disaster, of persecution
up ahead, the disciples all stuck by you to the end—or almost
to the end. There must have been such power in your words,
such magnetism in your very presence,
that they could virtually see
and taste and touch the kingdom you proclaimed, that they felt
themselves to be participating in it there and then.
And in that firm belief they faced whatever threats the kingdoms
of this world might raise against them; faced them not just
courageously but joyfully, rejoicing in the privilege
of sharing in your cross.

This paradox of joy that comes through pain,
this mystery that draws the highest ecstasy out of the depths
of agony, has illumined all the story of your church, Father,
has shone in its full radiance from the faces of the martyrs
from the beginnings until this very day and hour;
so that for them your cross, as has been written,
"is such a burden as sails are to a ship, or wings to a bird."

Lord, lead me to this mystery,
and grant me strength and depth in faith
that even I may share it.
                                        Amen.

EVENING

There are those, Lord God, who have told us down the ages
that to be chosen by you is to know automatic blessing;
is to receive rewards and guarantees in health and strength,
material prosperity in addition to eternal sure salvation.
There have been, and still are, persons who preach and hold out
promises of every problem solved, of all life's mysteries
unraveled, of miracle cures, checks in the mail, promotion,
family harmony, all granted freely to us now
if only we believe.

Yet this Beatitude of Jesus teaches quite the opposite;
suggests that the kingdom of heaven is linked with suffering
and persecution for the sake of righteousness. So too, Moses
and the prophets taught of a kind of chosenness, an election
that brought not privilege and power, special favors, and the like,
but the call to service, to self-surrender, to self-sacrifice.

It appears, Lord, that whereas some would say
religion rescues us
from all life's pains and problems, others tell us that religion
roots us firmly in the midst of all those problems.

Certainly your Son knew precious little
of the privilege of power in his life upon this earth.
His days of ministry were spent right at the aching heart
of this world's hunger, hurt, hostility. The blessings that
he knew and shared were blessings in the midst of disappointment
and despair, not a miraculous escape from all such sorrow.

Before I sleep tonight I think of fellow Christians
across the globe who share in this experience of our Lord,
who know imprisonment and torture for their faith; who suffer
joblessness, discrimination, ostracism just because they bear
the name of Jesus Christ; all who live
in mingled fear and faith, terror and trust in you.

Lord Spirit, speak to their spirits this night.
Grant them the reassurance that, even as they suffer,
they share the cross of Christ—and that those who share
the cross will wear the crown. Help me add to these prayers
whatever action I can take, financial, political,
personal, to bring such persecution to an end.
In the name of the crucified One I ask this, Lord.

Amen.

DAY TEN
Suffering for the Faith
Matthew 5:11–12

Blessed are you when others revile you and persecute you and utter all kinds of evil against you falsely on my account. Rejoice and be glad, for your reward is great in heaven, for so they persecuted the prophets who were before you.

MORNING

This Beatitude is different, Lord. It gets personal!
It doesn't only speak of types or categories of believers,
it addresses me directly and says, "Blessed are *you*. . . ."
And yet it doesn't seem to speak to me somehow,
at least, not to any "me" that I can recognize.

The fact is, I'm not unpopular enough to fit in here.
No one reviles me, really, or utters "all kinds of evil"
against me falsely. I get on well with others, on the whole;
and while I may not have that many bosom friends,
I think I'm generally well regarded, respected in my community.
Should I give all this up, seek to destroy my public image,
act deliberately in such a way as draws the scorn,
the condemnation, the rejection of my peers? But surely
self-made martyrs are not the kind you seek, Lord God.
Surely persecution is not something I can invite,
in order to reserve a front-row seat in heaven.

Perhaps an honest, searching look
at some of the many compromises on which
my present acceptability is based
is more like what you ask of me right here, Lord.
Would I, for instance, remain quite so popular,
quite so well thought of,

38

if, even in this "Christianized" society, I sought to live
in full the teachings of this Sermon on the Mount?

Suppose that I began to tell the truth—plain, unvarnished, clear,
direct and simple truth—
unembellished with the window dressing
and the weasel qualifiers of today. How would I do in business
or industry, or in the professions, even in the church
for that matter? Suppose, again, I took a stronger personal stand
on racism, sexism, unemployment, and poverty;
did all that I could,
in my job and in my community, to refuse to go along
with ugly prejudice, to advocate the cause of peace,
to provide jobs for people eager for the dignity of work.
Would I be seen as quite so amiable, such a regular guy?
Would this affect my reputation, job security,
promotion prospects,
and the like? Would I begin to know a little of the blessedness
of suffering for the faith?

It seems there *is* a way this saying speaks to me, after all,
this morning, Lord. Help me to think about its implications
for my life, my work, my attitudes, my relationships.
Then support me with the courage of my convictions.

Amen.

EVENING

I believe there is a way in which this saying
reaches out and touches every life, no matter what
its circumstances, Lord. One does not have to be
physically oppressed, imprisoned, tortured, to suffer
for the gospel's sake. Your will for every life,
every relationship, is love. It is love bears our fulfillment.
Love can restore us to the bliss of our original creation;
in fellowship with you, Lord God, and with
our fellow creatures.

But there is suffering, yes, even a certain martyrdom,
as an inevitable part of sharing love. This love is not,
at least for most, an easy, spontaneous, ecstatically natural
condition. My love has all too often lost its way
in the jungles of possessiveness, of jealousy,
of vanity and pride. Love, after all, demands humility—
the recognition and acceptance of my need for other persons
and for you, Lord. And I find that difficult to handle.
Love also hurts, brings pain, disappointment, even dread.
If I hold back my love, refuse to share it,
then I am much less threatened by
"the slings and arrows of outrageous fortune,"
the ever-present chance of accident, disease, and death
that, otherwise, could rob me of my beloved and my peace
of mind and heart. Much safer not to love at all.

Again, if I love, I will love another person,
another human being who is probably just as caught up
in pride, as twisted up by motivations as myself.
This can create a dreadful tangle, can lay bare
a veritable minefield of emotions.
We hurt ourselves in love, we your inept, imperfect children.
At times we act like cacti forced into a close embrace.
Even with the best intentions, Lord, we injure one another,
trample, tread upon such tender ground that the pain
can far outweigh the pleasure; that, at times,
we want to run and hide, cut ourselves clean off from love
with all its messy complications. Yes, Father,
we "persecute" each other and are "persecuted"
just because love makes us vulnerable, compels us
to reveal, expose our fragile inmost selves.

40

The secret here, you tell me, lies in not giving up,
not selling out to all the dreary games of selfishness
and sulking; but struggling to stay open, to be forgiving,
to stay gentle both to self and to the selves who touch my life.

And more than this, you tell me to be joyful.
"Rejoice and be glad"; those were the words of Jesus.
Help me to see the sufferings and sacrifice of love as
serving you, as building up your kingdom, Lord.
And in all this grant me joy.
                                   Amen.

DAY ELEVEN
Salt of the Earth

Matthew 5:13

You are the salt of the earth; but if salt has lost its taste, how shall its saltiness be restored?

MORNING

Lord Jesus, you used this striking image several times—
this metaphor of salt that loses flavor. It seems to represent
the Christian life, a life which, at its best, adds much
to the society around it. Salt preserves: and so the church
can act in desperately changing times to hold fast
eternal values, timeless truths, and teachings; to resist
the swiftly passing fads and fancies and stand firm
for love of God and love of neighbor.

More than this, salt fights against corruption,
acts as an antiseptic upon wounds. So must we, the church,
exert a cleansing, purifying influence,
not by judgmental posing but by our own example
of integrity and honesty, straight dealing
and trustworthiness to all that we encounter in a world
where such things trade upon the open market.

Salt flavors, Lord, lends life, color, zest to all it touches,
so our lives should be a source of gladness, vision, hope,
yes, even gusto, to a jaded world. This parable tells me, Father,
that wherever life begins to dance,
in art and music, fun and games,
in new discovery and rich old wonder and tradition,
wherever people leap to greet the moment with a song,
there is the salt of life.

And if I am not there, then I have lost my birthright,
given up my saltiness.

But most of all this parable of yours, Lord Jesus,
issues forth a warning; states that if we Christians are not
what we are supposed to be, do not preserve the very best,
add flavor, and resist corruption and decay,
then God will cast us out
and seek new salt with which to serve his world.

Lord, as I go forth into this day, renew for me
your vision of my saltiness; that whatever else I do
or fail to do today, I may bring flavor, sparkle,
interest, excitement, life itself into all my endeavors.
So may I yet be worthy of that title you bestowed
so long ago—"salt of the earth."

Amen.

EVENING

When Jesus gave this title to his disciples, Lord,
it did not convey upon them any special dignity or honor,
any privilege or rank. Rather, it called upon them to be useful.
I remember reading somewhere, Father,
an ancient Roman saying,
Nil utilius sole et sale,
"Nothing is more useful than sun and salt,"
reinforcing this idea that to be "salt of the earth" implies
less an ornamental role, more a utilitarian one.

Salt has been used in many ways: to cleanse, preserve,
add flavor, and the like. One further use, however, seems
suggestive for the church and for my life.

That is the use of salt to provide better traction.
Salt is spread, in winter storms, to melt the ice
on sidewalks, driveways, highways
to keep people from falling and help them move ahead.

Salt helps folk get a grip on things. In these slippery,
treacherous times, when so much appears to be in flux, all values
called in question, old moral standards seen as merely relative,
the arbitrary products of one culture in one era—in times
like these, society has a desperate need for traction:
for some place, some institution to hold firm
against the slide down into darkness
and the chaos of despair.

Human lives can serve this function too,
can act as hand- and footholds on the slick-sheer ice
of modern life, so that others, grasping firm, can regain
their equilibrium, can begin to move ahead, even
to walk again toward the future.

Lord, grant to me such wholeness and such wisdom,
such compassion and true charity, that I might provide
friction in this way, that I might be, for others, at least
a momentary resting place, a way to regain balance.

In such simple yet essential usefulness,
let me live out my call to be "salt of the earth."

Amen.

DAY TWELVE
Light of the World
Matthew 5:14–16

You are the light of the world. A city set on a hill cannot be hid. No one lights a lamp and puts it under a bushel, but on a stand, and it gives light to all in the house. Let your light so shine before others, that they may see your good works and give glory to your Father who is in heaven.

MORNING

Identity, Lord, is such a complex thing to grapple with.
"Who am I? What am I here for? Am I really anything at all?"
So often I feel just like a number—social security, zip code,
bank account, telephone, credit card, driver's license,
or whatever.
So many of the processes of daily life, procedures I cannot avoid,
reduce me to a printed set of digits on a slip of paper,
or, even worse, to holes punched in a card. And so
identity, for me, becomes non-entity.

You offer an alternative here: an identity, a sense of worth,
a purpose, even a mission that appears, at first, to be absurd.
After all, you spoke these words to rough, unlettered fishermen,
gathered in one corner of an obscure little portion
of the Roman empire. Surely Rome, that grand imperial city;
surely the emperor himself was where the light came from
in those days. So too with me. How can one minor,
insignificant sinner be described as being "light of the world"?

You also called yourself by this same title, Jesus, Lord.
John writes of you as saying, "As long as I am in the world,
I am the light of the world," and this helps clarify your call
to the disciples and to me. For although you are no longer
"in the world," you are still, for me, the Source of light.
Therefore my role is that of a reflector. My light

45

consists in holding and then passing on to others, best as I can,
the full and radiant beams still streaming from your life,
your death, your risen, living presence. My identity
is found, then, not in some brazen, garish self-projection,
but in the daily call to follow where you show the way.

So be my guiding light this day, Lord Jesus Christ.
And may your light shine through me
to illuminate the paths of others.

Amen.

EVENING

Light exists in order to be seen, to share itself with all around.
Its being is its purpose; it cannot help but be itself
and thus be radiant, bright, illuminating.

So too, my faith, Lord God, if it be genuine,
must be seen and known and recognized by others for what it is;
your presence and your grace—a burning lamp of love
set deep within. There are no options here; no either/or.
Faith does this, shares itself, by very nature.
Someone has written,
"There is no such thing as secret discipleship.
For either the discipleship destroys the secret, or the secret
destroys the discipleship." And I know this to be true
within my own life, Father. When I try to hide my faith,
to cover up the flame, it flickers and grows dim.

Thirty years ago, on entering the Royal Air Force, I made a vow.
I decided to continue kneeling, as had been my custom,
beside my bed in prayer every night. In a crowded barracks hut—
forty men from every walk of life—this provoked some

scornful comment, some mild belligerence, especially at first;
but soon a grudging new respect—not for me, I trust, but
for the faith they found in me—and finally a series
of encounters, discussions, one-on-one and in small groups,
that led me on, through ordination, to this evening hour
of prayer and meditation here tonight.

Lord, for all the ways your light has shone in me,
I thank you here and now. Let it continue to beam forth,
not only in the church but, above all, for the world, for this
was clearly your intent in these two parables of salt and light.
Do not permit me, then, to hide my faith under the bushel
of my parish, even of my home and family. Rather, let my life
reflect your glory in community and workplace, in politics
and business, in friendships and in leisure-time pursuits.

And grant that those who see may marvel, not at the lamp
but at the shining; and give praise and honor
to your holy name.
                        Amen.

DAY THIRTEEN
The Law and the Prophets
Matthew 5:17–19

Think not that I have come to abolish the law and the prophets; I have come not to abolish them but to fulfill them.

MORNING

When you said these words, Lord Jesus, people must have been
accusing you of trying to tear down the holy scriptures.
They must have seen your life, your flagrant disregard, at times,
for all the dim minutiae of religious law, the vast elaborations
of the Word worked out for centuries to govern every aspect,
every moment of one's daily life. They must have noted
just how you cut through those pettifogging regulations
in order to renew, restore, and heal the broken human lives
that came to you for help. And thus their accusation
that you would destroy the law and the prophets,
what today we call the Bible.

There are those who would destroy the Bible in our time, Lord:
secular powers who, through ignorance,
or by regarding this great book
as mere sectarian propaganda, would neglect its teaching,
trade in its glorious inheritance
for the latest, up-to-datest mess of pottage,
rob our children of the rich and splendid roots of Western culture
and send them, ignoramuses, into the worlds
of music, art, language, and literature
cut off from the deep wellsprings of their own civilization.

There are misguided Christians, too, Father,
who would "modernize" the faith

to such degree that, once again,
the wondrous heritage of scripture is denied our children
for the sake of pablum nature tales of butterflies, flowers,
falling leaves.
Then there are those who publicly embrace this book,
who clasp it to their bosoms with a fervor that impresses
all who watch, until they notice that this grasp is one
that squeezes out the lifeblood—all the laughter, the variety,
the majesty and mystery—and extracts, instead, some narrow,
cold, simplistic set of rules and regulations for
their own brand of salvation.

Lord God, I thank you that this Bible is a book of life,
not death; of faith, not fear; a book that can rejoice in all
the splendor of your spectacular creation, not flee from it
in puritan rejection, grim despair. Help me to found myself
deep in its depths, to soar at times to its lofty heights,
to learn from you how to fulfill and not destroy
its vast, resplendent Word of Life.

Amen.

EVENING

That word "fulfill," Lord, is a rich and fertile word.
It paints a verbal picture for me of what you meant to say here.
This picture is of fullness, of amplitude, of generosity
almost to overflowing.

I look at your life, lived here in our midst, Lord Jesus,
and I see fulfillment in the flesh. You did not only study the law
and teach the law—the scribes and Pharisees did that,
and you saw it was not enough.
You did not merely study the law and the prophets,

you fulfilled them; filled out those age-old sayings,
stories, teachings, poems, and the rest with the real stuff
of your own life.

Yes, Lord, you poured yourself, in all the fullness
of your Godhead and your manhood, into the shape and form,
the thrust and purpose of this ancient Book of books
and filled it full—full-filled it—lived it through and through
in teaching, healing, feeding; in bearing, suffering, dying;
yes, in rising from the dead to show me, teach me, set before me
in living, breathing, loving power the grace of God the Father,
poured out, poured into life for me, for all,
in all God's fullness.

And that, I see, is just what I am called to do in my time:
not so much to worship this old Book, but to use it;
not to treasure it, but to live it; to seek each day its wisdom
for the ways that I will tread; to come to know its themes,
its promises, its warnings so that they permeate the very way
I view reality; to discover in its pages, not the answers
to all questions, but the questions there that you would ask of me.
These may be questions that disturb, even disrupt; but they are
also questions in the lifelong answering of which I can begin
to walk the pathways of your kingdom, Lord,
the very avenues of eternity.

Lord God, I thank you for this Book and for the life—
tragedy, mystery, victory—
that is packed close within its pages. Guide me,
now, to taste that life, to find therein my daily bread,
true sustenance for the spirit; and by that food to walk
the ways of love, of grace, of peace,
through Jesus Christ—the Living Word.
                                                    Amen.

DAY FOURTEEN
Supreme Righteousness
Matthew 5:20

For I tell you, unless your righteousness exceeds that of the scribes and Pharisees, you will never enter the kingdom of heaven.

MORNING

At first this seems a quite impossible demand, Lord Jesus,
to go beyond the righteousness of scribes and Pharisees,
those dedicated men who spent their whole lives—
every hour of every day—in the punctilious observation
of innumerable laws derived from scripture.
To exceed such a remarkable performance
is beyond my human capability, the powers of my will,
my mind, my soul.

It has been argued that these men were legalists;
that in the thickets of their multiplying laws
they soon lost sight of you, and of your holy will, Lord God;
spent their lives pursuing such restricted and restrictive goals
that they never found true faith.
Yet their achievement was and is a wondrous one.
Their devotion to your will is, at its best, a truly holy thing.
And I am in no position to cast judgments on the quality
of other persons' faith. You, yourself, Lord Christ, held
their devotion up before me as a goal to be surpassed.

I find a legalism, too, within my own belief,
my Christian life of faith. I see it, for example, in my praying,
when my daily drawing near to you, O God, loses its joy,
its spontaneity, becomes a ten or fifteen, twenty-minute ritual
of words and postures, readings undertaken

out of habit or of duty,
even a false kind of insurance; trusting that the day will
surely bless me if I take the time to bless you at its opening.

Protect me, Lord, from all kinds of legalism.
Help me to stay open to your presence
and your promptings, Holy Spirit.
May the words I use in prayer be never solely words, but doors
that open up my hopes and dreads,
my loves, my failures and regrets
to you and thus provide an entrance also for your grace,
your strength, your judgment, wisdom, guidance for my days.

Thus may my righteousness at least approach, by grace,
those holy men of old. And in the mercy of your Son, my Savior,
may I be reckoned worthy of your kingdom, Lord.

Amen.

EVENING

What is this kingdom that you tell us how to enter, Lord;
into which I am permitted to proceed only by virtue of
exceeding righteousness?

The images of heaven that are a part and parcel of our culture,
Father, are not especially intriguing or inviting to me.
I could think of better ways to spend eternity
than sitting on a cloud in wings and halo,
strumming on a harp! Trumpet, anyway,
is more my instrument—I wonder whether Gabriel might
ever need some help. In short, Lord, heavenly bliss

has never struck me as my cup of tea, has always seemed
more boring than beatific.

However, in the Gospels, I can find another picture—
or, rather, other pictures, for you paint so many, Lord.
You spoke of heaven there as a wedding feast or banquet,
as a sheepfold or a family farm, a great tree filled with birds,
a precious jewel or a mansion house with many rooms.
And there are times, Lord Jesus, when you speak of heaven,
of the kingdom, not as something far away beyond the skies—
a place reserved for blessings after death—but rather
as a present possibility, as a state that can be entered here
and now. You told us that the kingdom is "at hand";
and that surely means close by, within my grasp
when I reach out in faith.

Might it be, Lord, that whenever I can act in loving-kindness,
can share my life with others, can stay receptive to your call,
can respond to human need, can free myself from all the clinging
chains of self and fear and pride, worthless ambitions,
then I will know at least a foretaste, a brief but tantalizing
appetizer of that feast that is to come, that banquet table
of the Lamb? Even so, Lord, teach me how to recognize
your kingdom when I glimpse it in this life.
And when I recognize it,
show me how to claim it by your grace.

Amen.

DAY FIFTEEN

Anger

Matthew 5:21–26

You have heard that it was said in ancient times, "You shall not kill.
. . ." But I say to you that every one who is angry . . . shall be liable
to judgment.

MORNING

Murder, in most societies, is accepted as the ultimate of crimes,
and often punished with the ultimate of penalties.
Here you point to anger with equal condemnation, Lord.
You remind me that, while killing is not an act I'm likely
to engage in, my anger can and does do violence,
almost every day.

There are the sudden flare-ups when I'm tired,
worried, frustrated, and then lash out with angry words,
often against the very ones I love the most—would want to hurt
the least. Such tantrums, all the same, are often just as quickly
gone as they arise. Wise families will excuse or overlook
most of them, make allowances for trying circumstances,
seek to swallow harsh retorts and cool things down awhile,
until apologies can surface to undo the tangled knots
and restore a basic harmony.

Resentment, bitterness, and grudge: those angers with a long,
slow-burning fuse are much more deadly, Father,
more destructive
of my peace of mind, my health, my spiritual welfare.
Burns, the poet, describes someone as
"Nursing her wrath to keep it warm,"
and I know exactly what he means because
I've lived it for myself.

There is a sweet and cloying comfort to be found in
grievance cherishing, in spending days and months, even years
in sullen, sulking, brooding rage. It can cultivate a just
and righteous feeling, the clear conviction that one is suffering
for a cause, a principle, a moral point that must not be conceded.

And yet, such anger can be fatal; devastating to marriages
and friendships, promoting stress and tension, the onset
of disease. Such anger kills just as surely, if not as swiftly,
as a knife or gun or bomb.

Help me to recognize my anger, Father,
even those long-suppressed hostilities and hurts that cripple me,
make misery for my neighbor. Then lead me into life that is
so radiant with your presence, so elevated with your grace
that all bitterness is washed away.
In Christ the Lord of life I pray.

Amen.

EVENING

The names we call people concern you in this saying, Lord.
Whereas, for me, this is a less than critical concern.
"Sticks and stones will break my bones,
but names will never hurt me" is a folk rhyme that we learn
in early childhood and generally seem to agree with.
People call each other all kinds of names these days, Lord Jesus,
and don't seem to take it all that seriously. Invective
is regarded as an art form, while casual curses
punctuate our movies and TV shows.

As I read your warning here, Lord, it strikes me that
it's not the names you condemn, but the attitude that lies beneath;
the supercilious contempt in which one can spit out the words,
"You fool!" Contempt is such a satisfying feeling,
such a smug, superior, self-satisfying thing.
It is a weed that flourishes in many kinds of soil.

There is the snobbery of social rank and class and station,
as if one could claim credit for the circumstances of one's birth.
Wealth and fine possessions can breed a sick and sneering
disregard for persons who are shut off from such privileges.
While the contempt of learning and of intellect for those
who are less educated, less sophisticated, can be the emptiest
of all. Surely the first and finest fruit of wisdom is
to realize the depth of one's own ignorance.

You died for all of us, Lord Jesus; on the cross
you bore the sins of wise and foolish, rich and poor,
peasant-born and noble. How dare I bear contempt for anyone
for whom you died? How can I sneer at others when my own sins
are so evident; when my sneering is so obviously a way to hide,
to cover up my failures from myself?

Forgive me, Lord, and set me free from my contempt,
that I may never have to hear you say,
"I never knew you."
Amen.

DAY SIXTEEN
Lust
Matthew 5:27–30

You have heard that it was said, "You shall not commit adultery." But I say to you that any one of you who looks at another lustfully has already committed adultery in your heart.

MORNING

Both these emotions, Lord, anger and now lust,
can and often do take me by surprise, so that I have little or no
control over their onset. And this is not, for the most part,
a gentle, gradual experience. In far less than an instant,
Lord, I can know lust in all its full and fierce intensity.
Is it not, then, an instinct, Father; a fire within
that reaches back to a more primitive me and is connected
with the essential urge to propagate, the preservation
of the species? But then how can I be judged for something
over which I have so little real control?

I recall that Martin Luther, on the topic of temptation, said:
"You cannot stop birds flying over your head,
but you can prevent them from nesting in your hair."
It is the nesting that I suspect you are concerned about.
The birds fly over, the thoughts and impulses enter my mind
willy-nilly; but I do not have to invite them to settle down
and make themselves at home.

My world is saturated with such traps, such pitfalls, Lord,
of sexuality. Books and magazines, films and billboards,
even the daily newspaper all encourage me to toy with,
yes, to entertain such thoughts. Sex nowadays seems almost
an obsession, used, perverted, prostituted in countless ways
to sell things to me, to attract my raw attention like

a carrot for a donkey, a red rag for a bull. I suppose
I should resent being treated like an animal in heat;
but all too often, Lord, it works, and I am caught despite myself.

Father, forgive my abuse of your gift of sexuality,
my mindless lack of self-control, my foolish, vain imaginings.
Help me to begin, at least, to move toward your purity,
a purity which does not have to be monastic, ascetic, or asexual,
but which expresses and enjoys my sexual being within
the context of honest, responsible, and appropriate
relationships. Let my sexuality hold much more in it of love
than of lust. Cleanse my mind and body. Fit them for
the presence of your passionate yet purifying Spirit.

Amen.

EVENING

"If thy right eye offend thee, pluck it out and cast it from thee."
I have heard, Lord, there are Christians who have done just that,
have obeyed this saying absolutely literally, maimed themselves
for life, rather than risk the possibility of transgressing,
and inheriting eternal condemnation.

Yet such drastic action would not necessarily solve the problem.
The seat of lust, the roots of such primeval motivations,
are not located in the eyes, the hands, or any other
portion of my anatomy, but in the mind, even the spirit,
which is turned away from you, Lord God,
and from your purifying presence.

May I, then, say that this is just a parable, merely
an analogy, not to be taken literally and therefore also
not to be taken seriously? But this kind of weasel thinking

is precisely what the analogy, this severe and surgical solution,
is designed to counteract. To decide, behind the secret screen
of mind and heart, that one would "do it" if one could
is not at all an ethically neutral act.
It has its consequences, soils the will
that forms such a decision, threatens, somehow, the integrity
of the person about whom I have entertained such thoughts
and idle dreams.

Your saying, at the least, demands that I should take
with deadly seriousness this whole matter of motivation;
this concern about the inner, unseen longings of my heart.
You command me, Lord, to excise from my mind, my lips,
my daily living even the contemplation of such acts, to guard
against, and crush when it arises, any motivation, vague intent,
half-formulated wish for infidelity. You set me on my guard
against the easy compromises, the convenient accommodations
I have made too often in the past; and warn me,
in no uncertain terms, about the consequences
of such loose imaginings.

Then, Lord, occupy my mind with your pure presence.
Occupy my hands with all the challenge of your love worked out
in action. Occupy my lips with the clean syllables of praise.
Be Lord over my life, and in ruling me rule out of me
all that is unclean, impure.
Fit me for your service, Lord.
Amen.

DAY SEVENTEEN
Divorce
Matthew 5:31–32

It was also said, "Whoever divorces his wife, let him give her a certificate of divorce." But I say to you that every one who divorces his wife, except on the grounds of unchastity, makes her an adulteress; and whoever marries a divorced woman commits adultery.

MORNING

"At least I try to live up to the Sermon on the Mount."
So many times, Lord, I have heard this statement,
or something similar, from persons—Christians or agnostics—
who have no idea what they are claiming;
who have obviously never considered, or even read,
these teachings and guidelines you set forth.
If they had done so, they would realize that the phrase
"at least" is in no way applicable here.
These ethical pronouncements, especially the teachings
on the Torah in which you heighten and interiorize
the demands of the old law, are severe, radical, stringent,
far beyond the reach of any casual believer,
even of most seriously committed Christians.

Your teaching on divorce surprises most of those
who read it nowadays. You set forth standards here
that can no longer be agreed upon, even among Christians.
For today, divorce has been accepted as,
in certain circumstances,
a valid Christian option: a responsible if regrettable
solution to impossible situations, to harmful
and destructive human relationships.

The scholars suggest, Lord, that when you spoke these words
divorce, in Israel, was a very simple matter,

60

a quite casual concern. It was limited to men,
of course, and all they had to do
was specify some "unseemly thing"—
no more defined than that—
and then formally reject their wives, because of it,
in the presence of two witnesses.
Your teaching on divorce protected women
from this cruel practice,
would have ruled out all such frivolous proceedings,
made divorce, except on serious grounds, impossible.

In an era such as this, when TV stars rewrite
their wedding vows to state, ". . . We will live together
as long as we both shall love," and the number of divorces
sets new records every year, perhaps we need to hear again
your call to full, lifelong commitments;
to the long and difficult road of forgiveness, reconciliation,
and renewal; to the understanding that we grow
through pain and stress and conflict maybe even more
than in times of tranquil bliss; and that to flee from these
too soon can be to flee from life itself.

Help me, Lord, to understand that marriage
is no fair-weather plant, which wilts and dies at the first touch
of winter's chill. That love is to be sought and found
right at the heart of all the weariness of stress
and disagreement, of mutual wear and tear,
of struggling to cope with the full range
of possibility and problem that is encountered within
normal family life. Deliver me from grasping after quick-fix,
cheap solutions. Unwind for me the strong yet tender cords
of life-lasting affection and respect. Then bind up
my broken hopes and dreams with them
and send me whole into this day.

Amen.

EVENING

Lord, despite the need today for more commitment,
there are still those I know—colleagues, friends, family—
for whom divorce has had to be the last resort,
the lesser of two evils, the only way to survive after
a terrible, life-shattering mistake.

Others, close to me, whom I respect as fellow Christians,
have remarried and, in many cases, built strong and loving
second homes and families. I cannot bring myself,
on the basis of this teaching, to judge these friends,
condemn them, for seeking to reclaim themselves
from a dreary living death.

But then, you would not have me judge, Lord Jesus.
Indeed, in this entire passage of your sermon,
you judge divorce severely, to be sure, but no more so
than my anger—"Whoever says 'You fool!' shall be liable
to the hell of fire"—or even what we used to call
"immoral thoughts." In this teaching on divorce
you delineate an ideal for Christian living, not a law
to be enforced. You are giving me a sublime goal
toward which my life should aim itself.
You are not legislating for society at large.

Looking again at this whole section on the law,
I realize that the basic sin in all these sayings is
the lack of love. The examples that you give me are symptoms
of that lack, and like hatred, anger, lust, divorce is also wrong;
falls far short of your perfect will for all your children.
It is an act of failure, of defeat; a human disaster of true pain
and lasting injury. So that even when it has to be,
when, tragically, no other alternative will serve,
divorce can never be regarded lightly, casually,
or with indifference. All of your children, Lord,
are found to be wanting in the light of the perfection
Jesus sets forth here. But the fullest message of the Gospel
holds that your vast mercy is more than sufficient
to cover every failure, every accident, mistake,
and blunder along the way to love.

Through repentance, forgiveness, restoration, Lord,
teach me to rebuild broken relationships wherever possible.
When this proves an impossibility, give me the honesty
and courage to accept my failure and move on
to build a newer, stronger framework somewhere else.
Thus may I yet turn failure into promise, turn hopelessness
and bleak despair to trust, that your grace may still
know victory in me.
                    Amen.

DAY EIGHTEEN
Oaths
Matthew 5:33–37

Again you have heard that it was said in ancient times, "You shall not swear falsely, but shall perform to the Lord what you have sworn." But I say to you, "Do not swear at all."

MORNING

O Lord my God, I must confess that your name
is far more often on my lips than your reality is in my thoughts,
your presence acknowledged in my heart and soul.

There appears to be a need in people to take holy things,
words of great significance and power, and employ them
in their daily speech as if, in doing so,
they add importance, impact, authority.
Yet all too often the opposite is what occurs.
The sacred becomes meaningless, a figure of speech,
habit, verbal blip that merely fills in space or time,
and we are left impoverished, not just in speech
but in our very souls.

I do this, Lord, in empty prayer: hurrying through
the dry and routine rituals of a daily discipline rather than
setting time aside to free myself for quiet contemplation,
true devotion. I do this also in expressions that I use
so mindlessly, habits of speech I have picked up so carelessly
that now, even as I see what I am doing, saying, implying
by these words and phrases, I have great difficulty
erasing them from the patterns followed by my lips
in casual conversation.

I wonder just how serious this is, Lord.
For even those who manage to rule out all such expressions
tend to rely, at least as heavily, on semi-laundered substitutes—
"For goodness' sake!" or "Oh my gosh!"—
that hardly even fool a little child, let alone
your majesty and wisdom. And this seems to be
a pattern that holds true in other languages and cultures,
in other eras of our history and literature.

Is there a sense in which blasphemy,
by its very nature, at least acknowledges your presence,
your existence, Father; at least recognizes and affirms your claim
on all of life, even in the act of seeming to deny it?
Perhaps, rather than attempting to cut out
such forms of speech, I should be trying to affirm them,
to own them; and even more, to speak them in full,
deliberate consciousness of all that they imply.

Lord, let my speech, my silence,
my deeds and actions, my inactions, proclaim this day
your presence throughout all my life,
your power for all living.
                    Amen.

EVENING

The basic issue here is that of honesty and truth.
Jesus' concern, it would appear, was not so much
with blasphemy as with the lying human heart
that would manipulate your name, Lord God,
for purposes of trickery and deception.

Jesus tells us a plain "yes" or "no" should be enough;
that an honest life and character are all the testimony
one could ever need or ask for. People seem to think,
on the other hand, that if they employ your name,
invoke the word for God in an agreement or transaction,
then you become a partner in the deal, and the whole thing
appears more trustworthy, more reliable.

When will I learn, Lord God,
that you are already partner to all deals,
that you take part in each and all relationships,
and that no contracts, treaties, covenants can be signed,
sealed, or delivered—whether or not your name is mentioned—
in which you do not have an interest, over which
you do not rule in truth and justice.

This life you give me, God,
is not a ship with watertight compartments,
into each of which I can decide whether or not to bid you
welcome by the invoking of your name. Your gift of life
is all one piece, Father. The language I use in church
should be no different from the words I speak at work.
The behavior, standards, attitudes for one
must be the same throughout. Everything I say and do—
my words, my promises, my deeds—take place in the full light
of your eternal presence, Lord my God.

In view of this, there can be no deceit;
and swearing in your name is mere redundancy.
Lord, remold my speech, but even more my life
to reflect the fact that you are always present;
and let my "yea" be "yea," my "nay" be "nay,"
the clear, transparent truth of Christ my Lord.
                                                    Amen.

DAY NINETEEN
Revenge
Matthew 5:38–42

You have heard that it was said, "An eye for an eye and a tooth for a tooth." But I say to you, "Do not resist one who is evil."

MORNING

"Eye for an eye . . . tooth for a tooth" seems pretty bloodthirsty
to me, Lord God. The whole idea of coolly and deliberately
removing someone's eye or cutting off a hand or foot
in the name of justice makes my blood run cold.
But then I learn that this was actually a great leap forward
in the history of law. This *lex talionis,*
as it is called, set up a limit to the vengeance
that had been limitless heretofore, so that,
instead of endless blood feuds, vendettas,
countless violent deaths because of some small insult
or offense, revenge was strictly limited, precisely
proportioned to the scale of the initial crime.

Yet Jesus saw that this was not enough. You taught us
through your Son that vengeance calls forth vengeance,
continuing the savage chain reaction of hatred, anger,
violence that has stretched down from the dawn of time.
The only way to break this bloody cycle,
this endless downward spiral—and Jesus saw this clearly
from the start—was to absorb the violence into oneself.
It was to receive in one's own body the cruel blows of anger,
bitterness, and pride and then refuse to pass them on,
refuse to be a link in the ancient chain
of retribution and revenge.

And thus, at last, the chain was broken.
We were set free in him: free, by following your Son's example,
to step clear out of the dreary, dismal circle
of revenge upon revenge, grudge after grudge,
hurt heaped on hurt in endless satisfaction;
free to step into the circle of your all-forgiving grace.

Deliver me, this day, from all the childish attitudes
that revolve around revenge: the grudges, spites, and vanities.
Let my words and actions serve today
to neutralize at least a fraction of the accumulated anger
of this world. Thus may I follow him who took our hostile pride
upon himself, bore it up upon the cross, and cast it down
to break its power once for all.

                                    Amen.

EVENING

It seems an awful lot for you to ask of us, Lord God,
to turn the other cheek, to go the second mile, and all the rest.
I mean, it really wouldn't work, Father,
if the police tried this, or the law courts, the prison guards,
or, even worse, the army. Such a policy,
if widely carried out, would quickly bring on anarchy,
put the whole world entirely at the mercy
of an unscrupulous few dictators of the Hitler-Stalin type,
or so it seems to me. Surely your people have a duty
to resist the powers of tyranny and evil,
not to stand by and let them ride roughshod
across the earth: at least that's what the Reformers,
the Founding Fathers of the USA,
and many others have believed.

And yet, to be completely fair,
the history of striking back, the long and weary record
of retaliation, is not all that impressive either, Lord.
For retaliation never seems to go unanswered.
It is responded to in kind, soon or late, and usually
with a little escalation added in.
So your children climb the ladder, that ladder which begins
in childhood's games and ends in nuclear holocaust.

Maybe I should worry less about police and prison guards
and start with my own life: my own relationships and rivalries,
enmities, grudges, spites. Maybe the problems
of the nations are not solved from the top down
but from the bottom up. Maybe if I, and other Christian folk,
would start to live this way and leave the rest of it—
the global scene—to you, things would work out.

One thing does seem clear. Hitting back
is not the answer. Getting even never got anyone very far,
one never stays even for long. Forgive me, Father,
for all retaliations, escalations, and the like
that have marred this day. Give me the faith
to live this teaching of your Son, my Lord,
and support me if and as I walk
with him the way to Calvary.
Amen.

DAY TWENTY
Perfection
Matthew 5:43–48

You, therefore, must be perfect, as your heavenly Father is perfect.

MORNING

What a discouraging, disheartening, yes,
thoroughly depressing piece this Sermon on the Mount can be!

Here I am, Lord,
struggling to observe the Ten Commandments—
to avoid robbery, idolatry, adultery,
too much coveting, and the rest—
and you tell me this is not enough . . .
nowhere near enough. Here I am, doing my best
to live a decent, respectable, law-abiding life—
avoiding all sorts of temptations, being a faithful spouse,
doing an honest day's work for my pay,
truthful (as much as is possible nowadays),
nonviolent (at least most of the time),
giving to charity (after all, I can deduct)—
and your comment is, "So what? Even the nonbelievers
do as much as that. You must be *perfect*."

Maybe I should give up right now,
quit while I'm far behind, decide this Christianity business
may be OK for preachers in their pulpits, Sunday mornings,
but is way beyond my kind of people, folk who have to face
the ugly real world Monday through Saturday.

Yet there is another word here besides "perfect,"
another key word in this text that might make all the difference.
That is the word "Father":
"perfect, as your heavenly *Father* is perfect."
And that second word clearly modifies the first.
I am to be perfect, then, not in any vague or general,
overall sense of perfection, but precisely in the way that you
are perfect, Lord my God. And despite all the attempts
of the medieval thinkers to spell out divine perfection,
to break it down in terms of "perfect essence, perfect form,
perfect knowledge, perfect power," and the like,
the Bible tells me you are perfect love.

That word "Father" itself points me to this.
It suggests that you are not a philosophical concept,
but the living, loving parent of the prodigal,
running out to greet your younger boy, embrace him, forgive him
all his foolishness, then reasoning—gentle but persistent—
with the older brother to bring him also back
within the restored family circle.

If this is the perfection that I am to strive toward,
then I am no longer so discouraged, so overwhelmed.
Such perfection still is well beyond my present power,
but it is a goal I can reach out for,
a fulfillment to be sought.
Even so, Father, guide me on my pilgrimage
toward this perfect goal today.

                              Amen.

EVENING

In all these teachings, Jesus Lord,
in all these probing reinterpretations of the law—
"You have heard it said . . . but I say unto you"—
you have been heightening the law's demands but also,
at the same time, deepening them.
You have sought to move our human understanding
of the will of God away from blind obedience to legalistic
written codes; to set it all, instead, within the heart,
within the all-encompassing embrace of love.

Yet love can be a slippery, evasive thing,
a convenient, covers-all-bases solution brought in
by preachers and such folk to tie things nicely with
a purple ribbon and avoid the hard-and-fast specifics
that I need to live my everyday existence.
To say that I "believe in" love,
to fervently assert "love is the answer"
when one hasn't even bothered to work out the question—
and, after all of this, to live no differently than before—
shows that the only thing I truly do believe in
is my own precious self.

You do not let me get away so easily, Lord.
You, in fact, are quite specific here. You point out
that love must show itself in the way I handle anger;
in the very names, the epithets, I fling about—
"You fool! . . . You idiot!"—and worse,
much worse. You tell me love is all wrapped up
with the way I control my sexual self; the way
I look at, think about, imagine persons of the other sex;
the way I relate to, cherish, care about
the one with whom I share my life.
And all this is most specific.

Love, you tell me, must govern what I say,
the things I am prepared to advocate, endorse,
things I will swear to. Love should guide me into
simple honesty and truth, away from all evasions, the standard,
accepted half-truths of these times. Love must remove
any and all desire for vengeance or violent retaliation;
must open me, not grudgingly or meagerly,

but with creative abandon to the needs of those about me;
must commit me to the work of making peace.

This, then, is the true perfection
that you set before me. And maybe this is harder,
more fearful and exacting than the overwhelming, vague,
and philosophical ideal I began with.
One thing is sure.
It will take a lifetime, more than most lifetimes,
to complete. And yet, that's what I'm here for.
That's what I'm here for, Lord.

Amen.

DAY TWENTY-ONE
Piety
Matthew 6:1

Beware of practicing your piety before others in order to be seen by them;
for then you will have no reward from your Father who is in heaven.

MORNING

If someone told me I was pious, Lord,
I'd be upset, worried, maybe even insulted.
Piety is not a virtue much sought after nowadays;
like righteousness, it seems to be increasingly restricted
in meaning to its more negative, selfish, insincere dimensions.

I tend to think of pious persons,
if I think of them at all, as goody-goody types—
quite otherworldly and irrelevant—whose chief concern
lies in the preservation of their spotless little souls;
and who, therefore, have no time or energy to spare
for the needs and hurts of other people.

It was not always so, Father.
Piety, devoutness, the leading of a pure
and holy life, has been, till recently, one of
the major goals of Christians. Perhaps this attitude today
is a reaction, a rejection of the sanctimonious portraits,
many of them caricatures, passed down to us
in literature from a previous age. Whatever the reason,
I would like to know the true meaning of piety, to recapture
at least a grasp of the outline, the broad and general
dimensions of Christian holiness, of what it means to be devout.

Could it be, Lord God, that this act
I am engaged in here and now contains the secret?
Might true piety consist, not in certain precious attitudes
and airs—a sort of weird and wispy aura: a gaze, both reverent
and detached, which focuses afar on vistas not revealed
to lesser eyes—might honest piety be found
through life that has its roots set deep in prayer?
Is holiness, perhaps, a flower that blossoms freely,
naturally, yet completely unself-consciously;
one of those goals which, if I aim directly at it,
I am sure to miss the mark, but if I focus close beside—
on practicing your presence, Lord, on living out your gift
of life for others—I will hit the target,
win the prize?

Lord, I know that I am called to live
a pious faith, a saintly life. But if I ever do,
surprise me with it. Let my devoutness be a quality
of inner peace and strength from you, rather than
any conscious, forced attempt to appear holy.
This I ask through him whose authentic, winsome piety
made others follow, trust, and love him.

Amen.

EVENING

This matter of public piety, Lord Jesus,
is a troublesome concern. Earlier in this great sermon
you command your disciples to let their light shine forth
so that other people may see their good works
and give glory to the Father.
Yet, right here you say "Beware" of such activity.

I can begin to grasp some of the dilemma,
the tugging in opposite directions by mixed
and mingled motivations, when I look at what happens
in public life today. Well-known figures,
politicians and the like, even Presidents, take part
in various religious acts. And such events are widely publicized.
The question is: Are they doing what they do as sincere believers
making public witness of their deep personal faith
or are they merely seeking to gain votes?
It is a narrow line to draw, a very difficult
distinction to make clear. In truth, both motivations
may be present in the selfsame person and at
the selfsame time. I suppose that's why you said, "Beware!"
and issued so severe a warning here.

This problem, however, cannot be reserved
for those who lead the public, who seek after
their political support in one form or another.
It also affects me and my own life of faith.
It can often be quite helpful, advantageous, in the society
I live in, to be seen and known to be religious.
Not too seriously religious, you understand,
not zealous or fanatical in any shape or form,
but at least mildly so, acceptably committed,
"a fine God-fearing citizen"—that sort of thing.

And much of this is plainly unavoidable.
If I do not make a secret of my faith, strive to conceal
my beliefs and practices, then people have to know;
they cannot help but see. And from the point of view of witness,
evangelism, setting an example, calling attention to key issues,
such exposure is surely desirable, even essential.
The key to this apparent contradiction must lie
within the area of motivation. Indeed, you clearly state
that this is so, Lord Jesus, when you tell me to shine forth
my light so that all who see may "give glory," not to me
but to my Father who is in heaven.

Thus remind me, Lord, in all my witnessing,
that my goal is not to "do well by doing good,"
not to personally prosper from my public acts of faith;
but to direct the gaze of others toward you,
and to glorify your holy name alone.

                                        Amen.

DAY TWENTY-TWO

Almsgiving

Matthew 6:2–4

Thus, when you give alms, sound no trumpet before you, as the hypocrites do . . . that they may be praised by others. Truly, I say to you, they have received their reward.

MORNING

I read a novel once—a series of novels, in fact—
in which this theme of secret giving was developed
into a whole philosophy, a way of Christian life.
In brief, the author argued that, by elaborately secret acts
of generosity and kindness, acts in which the giver
had to be completely anonymous, even to the recipient of the gift,
one could not only follow our Lord's teaching
but also reap undreamed of benefits, in terms of happiness,
creativity, and other intangible rewards here in this life.

At the time, Lord, I found these novels quite inspiring.
Yet I have come to wonder about their message. After all,
if keeping one's gifts secret is merely a method
for guaranteeing happiness, success, however viewed,
then the whole scheme seems flawed with selfishness
below the surface.

Once again the question focuses on motivation,
as is the case with the majority of these teachings, Lord.
You are warning me that "doing the right thing" is not enough.
You are pointing out the danger of "the right deed
for the wrong reason." You propose—
and it does seem to add up according to
a kind of ethical arithmetic—that if I give
in order to receive the credit here and now,

the public recognition and acclaim that follow acts
of special generosity, then I should not look for credit
also from the Lord.

This reminds me of a practice which today
is known as double-dipping, Lord. And the teaching
does ring true for modern life, when so much
of what is charitably given is regarded as deductible from taxes.
Do I, then, practice double-dipping when I both deduct
my pledge and regard it as an offering to you?
I guess, again, the crux lies in the reasoning behind,
the motivation for the gift. If it is given, pure and simple,
for the purpose of avoiding taxes, then the answer
seems quite clear. But if my giving springs
from gratitude to you, then that is
quite another story.

I wonder too, Lord, about all those corporations
that make widely fanfared gifts. Are they only buying
advertising, engaging in some loftier type
of public relations scheme? And yet, the gifts do good.
They promote the public welfare, for the most part.
We, the people and society, would surely miss such contributions
if they ever were to cease.

I guess I would conclude, Lord, that, in general,
it is better that the right thing be done,
even for inferior reasons, than that it not be done at all.
But the way of true perfection, the fully Christian way,
is to make a gift not seeking a reward at all,
in heaven or on earth, but simply
for the sheer joy of giving,
and in gratitude to you.
                              Amen.

EVENING

Far from worrying over public versus private
acts of charity, Lord, my concern relates to this whole area
of giving. You stated, earlier, that I should give
not just my tunic but my cloak as well.
Scholars, those who know the customs of your time and place,
point out that generosity like that would leave
an average person—like many of those
to whom you spoke—completely naked.

My giving is a much more cautious thing:
perhaps a handkerchief, a tie, a shirt at most,
never a tunic, let alone my only cloak!
What I mean, Lord, is that despite your teachings, warnings,
my prayers, and professions of belief, I find it hard,
almost impossible, to sit as loose to the material world
as you would have me sit.

I worry too about the future, about the mortgage,
about my children's education and their health.
And while I realize that some of this concern is manufactured,
merely an excuse, yet the basic concerns there—
the desire to be responsible, to provide
for my family, to meet my obligations—
are not entirely self-indulgent.

I need your help, Lord Christ, to grapple honestly
and fairly with the dimensions of my stewardship
in this complex, modern world.
I suppose the place that I begin is right there
in that concept "stewardship": the basic understanding
that all I have, all I save, all I earn derives from you.

Perhaps if I could recognize this fact,
accept it as the nonnegotiable basis for my ownership,
then specific issues could be raised in true perspective;
no longer doling out how much I keep, how much
I give to God, but rather asking which, of all your gifts,
I need to hold for now, and which can be
returned in thankfulness.

Forgive my failures here, Lord God.
Guide me to the responsible fulfillment
of my stewardship through Christ
who gave his all for me.

Amen.

DAY TWENTY-THREE
Praying
Matthew 6:5–8

And when you pray, you must not be like the hypocrites; for they love to stand and pray in the synagogues . . . that they may be seen by others. Truly, I say to you, they have their reward.

MORNING

If your comments here were to be taken
completely literally, Lord, then public worship
might be abandoned altogether. But I cannot believe
your intention was to condemn all public prayer per se.
Your scorn here is expressed, as I understand the passage,
against ostentatious public praying; against prayers
that rise no higher than the lectern or the ceiling of the church;
against prayers that call attention, not to God,
but to the eloquence, the language skills, the mellow tones,
the whole demeanor of the one who actually speaks the words.
I have known such prayers, Lord,
and I am ashamed to realize that at times
I may have prayed them. But I have also been uplifted
to the throne of grace, found myself judged,
redeemed, strengthened, and sent forth
through the mystery and miracle of authentic public prayer,
and I am thankful for its ministry.

Your summons here, however, is to the private place,
the quiet time, the moments set aside in solitude
when I can be myself, and be with you,
and be restored to sanity and wholeness.
How I need such times, Lord Christ!
I remember from the Gospels how you drew aside,
how oftentimes the crowds or the disciples would come

81

seeking you and find that you were gone,
alone into the mountains,
to seek quietness in prayer and meditation.
And if you felt such a need, how much greater is my own?

And still I fool myself, try to avoid acknowledging
this need, say that I'm too busy, say I'll do it later
in the day, and so cut myself off from the deep wellsprings
that can quench my thirst, heal my hurt, bring purpose,
meaning, glory, even, to my days.

Forgive my foolishness, my cowardly refusal
to lay hold on all the life you offer.
And lead me to yourself, a lamb of your own flock,
a sheep of your own fold. Then hold me in your grace
this day and always, Lord.

Amen.

EVENING

Some people, religious professionals for the most part, Lord,
speak of prayer as if it is an easy, simple, natural thing,
an action that requires no special training, or preparation,
but can be effortlessly engaged in by any normal person.

And in one sense, Father, I suppose
that this is true. Prayer is talking to you:
telling you my needs, my fears, my failures, my dreams.
And there are moments—crises, especially, and emergencies—
when prayer is the most natural response of all.

It's not so much these prayers
that I have trouble with, Lord God, nor is it
the ones in Sunday morning service, for the most part;

they tend to be beyond my personal control.
It is the prayers I pray morning and evening
that cause problems for me . . . and the problem is
in what to say, the question of "vain repetitions."

If I use a prayer book, like this one, for example,
let its daily meditations guide and mold my spiritual life,
then prayer can come to seem secondhand,
based on someone else's thoughts, no matter how original
or well expressed those thoughts may be.
Again, the use of books like these can grow
to be mechanical, can develop into a formula
that must be read and "gotten through" before
the day can really start. Yet another hazard of these
books of prayers is that, in praying them,
one can get caught up in the language used, the style,
the images, and so on, and wind up not really praying,
but reading a good book—or criticizing a bad one.

On the other hand, if I vow that all my praying
will be completely personal, that every word I speak
to you, Lord God, will be original, uniquely mine,
the spontaneous expression of the moment, then I find myself
dug in to another kind of rut, another set of routine repetitions.
This is because my mind is not all that creative
on a regular day-to-day basis; left to find
something to say to you, I will usually come up with
the same old things again and yet again.

Help me to perceive, Lord, that prayer,
like every other relationship, is complex, multifaceted;
that there will be times and seasons when a prayer book
or guide is absolutely essential; yet, at other times,
no words but mine can fully plumb the depths,
soar the heights I reach in prayer.
Let me never become satisfied with "vain repetitions"
of any kind, my own mumblings or holy printed words
upon a page. Reveal to me the vast, rich storehouse of prayer,
both personal and universal, ancient and up-to-date.
And may I spend my days exploring all
its many rooms and doorways.

Amen.

DAY TWENTY-FOUR
The Model Prayer
Matthew 6:9–15

Pray then like this:

Our Father who art in heaven,
Hallowed be thy name.

MORNING

You gave us much to think about,
to explore, wonder at, direct our lives toward,
when you gave this model prayer, Lord Jesus.
As I read it over once again, I am reminded that you taught it
as a model: not just a set of sacred words to be repeated
till the phrases become blurred, lose their meaning
and their cutting edge. All our praying,
you suggest, might well be shaped around its two basic concerns:
around God and humankind.

You teach here, first of all, that God is Father
and at the same time Sovereign Ruler of the universe.
In these four brief opening phrases—

Our Father who art in heaven,
Hallowed be thy name.
Thy kingdom come,
Thy will be done,
On earth as it is in heaven

—is held together, captured for us once for all,
all the glory and the intimacy, the transcendence
and the immanence, the power and the passion, the justice
and the redeeming grace that thinkers have filled volumes
upon volumes attempting to explain.

You tell us that the personhood, the presence
which called and yet calls galaxies into being,
which devised the intricate timing of the atom,
the exquisite structures of the living cell, is also,
and above all else, loving; cares in a way far beyond
understanding for each created human life; and seeks,
down all the ways of history and science,
to win us and our love back to himself.

And if you had taught us nothing else but this,
Lord Jesus—shown us that somehow our envisioning,
our understanding, our experience of God from now on
must encompass not just the imagery of the royal court
(thrones, pomp, majesty, and might) but also must embrace
the deepest joys and pains of family, of parenthood—
then we would still be forever in your debt.
The devotion with which we cherish our first newborn;
the pride with which we watch our children grow as they crawl,
walk, talk, read and write, run and swim; the frustration,
agony balanced with the occasional ecstasy,
of guiding them through the years of adolescence;
the wonder as they emerge into full and splendid
adult independence—all this is now embodied within
God our Father and our Sovereign Lord.

This is a miracle, as much as any healing
you performed, Lord Christ. And as I pray these words
this morning, join countless millions across the globe,
countless generations down the ages, in saying them,
I thank you for their insight, their comfort,
and their power.
                    Amen.

EVENING

In this prayer for every age, Lord Christ,
you speak to us, instruct us, not only about God
but also about ourselves.

Three needs are now spelled out, three basic requirements,
as it were, for life:

> Give us this day our daily bread;
> And forgive us our debts, as we forgive our debtors;
> And lead us not into temptation, but deliver us from evil.

Food, then, forgiveness, and a future;
or, perhaps, provision, pardon, and protection . . .
three needs for being human.
"Our daily bread" reminds us we are human.
We are not spiritual beings, isolated souls, imprisoned
for a time in solid flesh; but we are living beings,
flesh and blood, whose physical daily needs are recognized,
are important enough to be named here first as
an essential part of God's provision for us.

This is an eminently practical prayer, Lord,
no theoretic musing on existence, but a clear, specific request—
a desperate request, in fact, by all too many still today—
for simple sustenance enough to make it
to another sunrise.
So much of your message was like this, Lord Jesus,
based in and around the most ordinary physical stuff of life:
a loaf of bread, a lost coin or wandering sheep,
a marriage or a job or the sowing of a field,
the catching of fish, the building of a house.
In all this you assure us that God cares about the details,
about whether or not we have food enough to eat.
Indeed, the Father has provided on this earth
more than sufficient to support all his children.
And so long as there are folk who still can pray
this prayer for daily bread in vain, then the rest of us,
God's children, are failing in our stewardship.
We deny, in this, the very prayer we utter here:
"Lord, thy will be done on earth as it is in heaven."

Which brings me to forgiveness—another basic need,
another affirmation of my humanness, bound to know failure
and defeat upon occasion, caught in the maze of life
that leads so easily to love of self, not God,
to fear of others and not trust,
to self-protection and not self-surrender,
to grudges, spites, and hurts that linger far too long
and block the healing paths for grace to flow
and cleanse and purify.
Your forgiveness, both given and received,
is a fundamental need as real as food to eat.

Finally, you teach us to pray for protection:
protection not so much from danger, want, or sickness;
these are all a part of life, after all.
The protection you encourage us to pray for
is safekeeping against evil. And I suspect you mean
by that, against the powers that would lead us to betray
our selves, to sell our very souls.
For if life is more than mere survival;
if integrity and justice, creativity and love—
the very qualities you teach in the Beatitudes—
are closer to the essence and the purpose of our living than
our comfort and physical well-being; then the greatest danger,
the only true, eternal threat, is to our spiritual selves.
You taught that we could save our lives and,
in the effort, lose our souls, Lord Christ.
This prayer seeks protection from that fate.

Then hear me, Lord, as in the closing moments of this day
I say, again, with renewed comprehension and with wonder,
the words you taught us to pray, saying . . .

                                              Amen.

DAY TWENTY-FIVE

Fasting

Matthew 6:16–18

And when you fast, do not look dismal, like the hypocrites, for they disfigure their faces that their fasting may be seen by others. Truly, I say to you, they have received their reward.

MORNING

Fasting, at least of the religious variety,
is a practice with which I am not all that familiar, Lord.
And I suspect that many Christians, perhaps most,
share this experience . . . or lack of it.
It used to be true that at least my Roman Catholic
sisters and brothers took this ancient custom seriously.
However, recent changes in that church have made fasting there
also a quite uncommon thing.

Interestingly enough,
while religious fasting has declined, as such,
fasting for other reasons, chiefly dietary fasting,
the practice of cutting down on food in order to lose weight,
seems to have been simultaneously on the increase.
Could it be that we are meant to fast:
and if we will not do it for one reason,
we will do it for another?

There have been occasions in my life—
few and far between, I fear—
when I have fasted for a cause or because of my convictions.
"Fasts for Peace" they were, or "Food Days,"
when people gave up eating to raise money for the starving
and to gain some sense of momentary sharing
in their burden. In recent years

I have tried fasting on Ash Wednesday or Good Friday,
at least during a portion of the day. And from such times
I have begun to discover something of the effectiveness
of disciplined times of self-denial.

Most commonly in the scriptures, fasting is seen
as part and parcel of repentance. Inasmuch as fasting
clears the mind and sharpens the perceptions,
I can see it does have value. But as repentance,
fasting smacks of showing God how sorry I can be;
and I'm sure that's not the kind of showing
God either asks for or responds to.

There is an old rabbinic saying:

> God will judge us for every permitted pleasure
> that we fail to enjoy.

And while fasting may have benefits in heightened
spiritual insight and in moral self-control, there is a sense
in which, taken to extremes, it may be seen as rank ingratitude,
the spurning of God's gracious cornucopia of gifts
offered to us in creation.

The truth will probably lie somewhere in between;
where fasting, coupled with deep prayer, honest reflection,
can shed light, bring forth new strength.
May I grow to understand and appreciate more fully
this ancient custom, Father, and to apply its lessons
to my pilgrimage of faith.

Amen.

EVENING

The question here, Lord Jesus,
is not "To fast or not to fast?"
In this saying you assume that I will carry on
this old, time-honored custom. The problem you raise here
is that of inauthentic fasting, of suffering for show.
You are opposed to fasting, just as you were
to giving and to praying, when it is done
for the sole purpose of impressing other people.

Nowadays, at least in Western culture,
people do not dishevel hair and clothing,
spread wood ashes on their faces to look pale,
so that the world may know that they are undergoing a fast.
Yet ostentatious suffering, sham sacrifice,
is still a very evident human foible.

I know that personally when I give up something
for my faith—shopping on Sunday, maybe, a game of golf
to go to church, finances in a pledge campaign, time and effort
in a worthy cause—I like people to know about it.
I want them to appreciate all that I am giving up.
Of course, I could always call it "witnessing,"
but somewhere deep inside I know the motive here is vanity,
sheer spiritual pride.

You warn me clearly, Lord,
that if what I want is credit, status from
my fellow men and women, people to think, and say,
that I am "wonderful" or "noble," "sacrificial," "dedicated,"
and the rest, then I will get just what I want.
No more, no less than that. But if I wish
to please the Lord, offer myself willingly to God
in sacrificial ways, I had better make no display of
my sacrifice. I had better find and share the quiet joy,
true joy that lies in Christian service.

Lord God, deliver me from phony suffering.
Let me never try to counterfeit my sharing in
your burden which you bore upon the cross.
Amen.

DAY TWENTY-SIX
Treasure
Matthew 6:19–21

For where your treasure is, there will your heart be also.

MORNING

What is it that I really, truly treasure?
What is there, in all of life, that I cherish
above all else? Your words about "treasure in heaven,"
Lord Jesus, make me ask such questions of myself, my life,
things I hold dear.

There would be no lack of answers
if I were to pick up the daily paper or a magazine,
turn on the television set. My world is filled with people,
institutions telling me what I should treasure,
what I should spend my life pursuing and, if possible,
amassing and enjoying.

Some would tell me to chase money and all that money buys:
the fine cars and clothes, the latest electronic marvels,
the boats and second homes and such.
Others will propose places to go, new things to see,
gala occasions to attend. Still others
will name health, physical fitness, as the one thing
to be treasured above all. Or how about prestige,
success, or sexual adventure?
Is there anything, Lord, among all these,
that I can truly treasure?

Suppose I were to turn your saying around
and say, "For where your heart is, there you will find
your treasure"? So much of what I do, seek after,
spend my time pursuing, does not really have my heart in it.
Oh, yes, the glittering prizes draw and hold my gaze.
I dream of all the possibilities for fun, profit,
advancement, stimulation they will bring into my life.
But all the time my heart, that "tell-tale heart,"
is telling me that it is not really in the chase at all.

I have sensed this once or twice before:
when I have managed to attain one of these goals,
won promotion, afforded some new product, gadget,
that I've lusted after over several months.
The initial thrill soon passes. The new-car smell wears off.
That lightened step in the height-of-fashion outfit
soon calms down to normal once again,
as whatever it was settles in, takes its place among
the other ordinary stuff of daily life.

But let a friend suffer an accident,
my spouse threaten the bond of intimacy I have taken
so for granted, my parents begin to show the signs of aging,
failing health, my child call home in tears,
and all at once things are clarified.
I know just where my treasure is;
my heart shows me the way. And VCRs and cottages
and trips around the globe and even jobs assume their proper
secondary role. I know that I would trade them all,
give them all away in an instant, if there could
only be a cure, if help was just available.

Yes, I treasure those I love, Lord.
My heart knows where my treasure is. And that love,
I trust, will guide me—guide us all, at last—to a place
"where neither moth nor rust consumes . . . where thieves
do not break in and steal." So lead me, Lord,
and guide me to my treasure.
                                        Amen.

EVENING

You shattered with your life, Lord Christ,
the false and empty treasures of this world.
You flung the gauntlet down, issuing a challenge
to everyone who said that treasure was something to be seized,
fought for and won by force of arms, bought by
the deep wide pockets, schemed after by the crafty strategists—
everyone, indeed, who claimed that treasure
was any *thing* at all.

You took on, disputed in your ministry,
the mighty hosts of Rome, the entrenched rituals
of the temple, the wealthy magnates of the marketplace.
You proclaimed to all these three—politics, religion,
economics—that they were secondary:
that, while good could come by them, they were not
the treasure trove that people yearned for,
the pearl of great price a person would sell everything to buy.

That was why they killed you . . . we killed you
in the end, because you told us, demonstrated to us,
that the treasure that we thought we owned was secondary.
Not necessarily evil, or bad for human beings;
not really worthless; but secondary to the power of love,
to our relationships to one another,
to our relationship to God.

"Treasure," you announced, as you strode the hills of Galilee,
"treasure is really truth, integrity, wholeness of body,
mind, and spirit." "Treasure," you proclaimed loud across
the towering battlements of Jerusalem, "treasure is courage,
the courage of your convictions, courage to live and die
for what you love, not what you want."
"Treasure," you gasped out between parched and bleeding lips,
"treasure is forgiveness issued in the very act
of cruel brutality." "Treasure," you decreed, as you
walked the Easter garden, "treasure is the certainty
that death and all its powers are conquered
once for all."

The other things all fade and die. That stuff
we think we can possess—hold on to, stuff into our pockets,
banks, wherever—will not, cannot last.

The only things eternal lie right here within
our easy reach, yet far beyond our grim, possessive grasp.
The solid rock of faith in God.
The moving ocean tide of God's full love
reflected in our human loves. The beauty, passing,
changing with the seasons, yet eternally present,
of this world in all its splendor. The sheer delight
of human creativity in art and dance and music,
poetry and laughter.

These are the treasures of our world,
treasures that you revealed in all the fullness of your life
and death and resurrection, Lord. Now direct my thoughts,
my prayers, my life toward them: that when the day
of resurrection dawns, I too may share
the glory of your rising.
                              Amen.

DAY TWENTY-SEVEN
Eyes and Seeing
Matthew 6:22–23

The eye is the lamp of the body. So, if your eye is sound, your whole body will be full of light; but if your eye is not sound, your whole body will be full of darkness.

MORNING

Who I am affects all that I see.
My basic personality, identity, will inevitably shape
my vision and experience of the world. In this parable, Lord,
of light and of the eye, you tell me this
and warn me of the consequences.

If I am, for example, a self-centered individual,
I will perceive the whole world about me only in terms
of how it may or may not serve my interests,
advance my personal satisfaction and well-being.

If I am a gloomy, pessimistic soul,
then everything and everyone I meet will serve
only to confirm me in my dreary, bleak opinions.

If I look through the narrow eyes of prejudice,
the persons I encounter will be seen by me,
not as they really are, in all their God-given individuality,
but as conforming to some ugly stereotype, as filtered through
some dark, distorted lens of fear and hatred.

If I see the world through jealous, envious spectacles,
then those who might have been for me companions, partners,
friends to share my load or know my helping hand,
are transformed into rivals, competitors,

those who seek to rob me of my rights, my just reward,
my fair share.

If anger is allowed to cloud my vision,
if a banked, slow-burning fire eats away at my insides,
a hostile world of tricks and treachery will be my habitat,
and provocation and betrayal will be everywhere I turn.

And if dollar signs dance forever
right before my eyes, then life and all its vast potential
will be reduced to buying and to selling,
to commodities for marketing. And death will be
a bargain I have grasped and gained in exchange
for my own soul.

Teach me to look at life, the world,
my fellow creatures through your eyes, Lord God;
to see this whole creation as you did when you completed it
and pronounced all you saw as not just "good"
but "very good." So may my eye be single,
clear, and true to you this day.
                              Amen.

EVENING

"Keep your eyes on the prize.
Hold on . . . hold on," so sang the slaves,
the black folk dragged from Africa to work and die in chains.
And their songs, their faith, their trust in you, Lord God,
have much to say to me tonight.

My eyes so often wander from the goal
you set before me; lead me off on detours,
side roads, even broad and gleaming avenues that promise
glittering destinations, yet eventually dwindle,
disappear in swamps and endless desert.

There is so much to gaze on in this world;
so many shining darknesses have uncanny power
to draw the eye, to fix it fast upon themselves,
and then absorb it deep within their vacant depths.

And it isn't all that easy, Lord, to gaze steadily at you.
At first, all I can see is a figure hung in agony
upon a cross. And that is not a pleasant or inviting prospect:
especially when that figure seems to be beckoning somehow,
to be calling, "Follow me," seems to be bidding me,
"Take up your cross." This is not exactly
what I had in mind when I set out across the flowered hills
of Galilee, when I responded to your call to build
a kingdom here on earth.

"I am the light of the world"
is what you told us, Lord. Am I, then,
to focus so completely upon you,
upon your wonder and your woundedness,
your tragedy and triumph, that everything I am and do,
say and live for, is permeated, bathed in,
flooded by your light?

Shine that light upon me now, Lord Christ.
May it watch over me throughout these hours of darkness
and illumine all my days. So may my eye be sound,
my whole body full of light.
                              Amen.

DAY TWENTY-EIGHT

Two Masters

Matthew 6:24

No one can serve two masters; for either you will hate the one and love the other, or you will be devoted to the one and despise the other. You cannot serve God and mammon.

MORNING

Maybe it is just that times have changed,
and life-styles, since those far off, less complicated days
when you spoke these words, Lord Christ;
but certainly today a statement such as this
would be inaccurate, even patently untrue.

People do it all the time: serve two masters, Lord.
And I don't just refer to those—and not a few—
who are holding down two jobs or even more.
The whole of life today, in this late twentieth century,
is a balancing act, a trading off, an equalizing process between
the demands, pressures, expectations, not just of two
but of a whole circle of masters.
"Multiple masters" would seem to be
more like the case for many people.

Most immediately, there are the competing claims
of both career and family; and there is just no way of choosing
one of these above the other; somehow they must be matched,
made to cooperate. But beyond and circling all around
these two there exists a host of others:
home and school, garden and church,
health and education and cultural stimulation,
the needs of my parents, the needs of my friends;
my social life, my comfort, relaxation, hobbies; and then

98

the world out there, community and city,
starving youngsters in Africa, innocent victims in Beirut,
politics and the threat of nuclear disaster.
"No one can serve two masters" did you say?
Lord, there's many a time I would be more than happy
to settle for only two.

And yet, when I stop to think about it,
in a deeper and more fundamental sense you may be right,
after all. There is a level far beneath all these
revolving priorities, concerns, where I ask myself what life
is really all about, what I am doing here, where I am going,
what I am making of my life: a level at which things
really do boil down to the choice of one
from two alternatives.

Put at its very simplest and starkest,
the choice you set before me is one between
the two most basic of realities. It is a choice of life
or death. "No one can serve two masters" means
I can be ruled by life or ruled by death. I can live my days
toward the grave, the tomb, the six-foot drop;
or I can raise my eyes and focus them beyond—toward eternity.

Make me aware, Lord God, of all the masters
who would claim me in this day I now begin. As I evaluate
their demands upon me, help me to see
which are the ones that lead to life in you,
and which would drag me down to dusty death.

Amen.

EVENING

To serve the powers of death is not
some melodramatic business of black magic, witchcraft,
covenants with Satan. For me, at least, it is a much more
commonplace, mundane affair. Essentially, Lord, I see it as
the conviction that life's goal lies in the grave:
that all existence moves toward oblivion,
dissolution, and the dark.

Shakespeare once wrote, "Death is a fearful thing . . .
to die, and go we know not where." And this fearful thing
affects the life it dominates. The life lived toward death
is a life bound fast in fear. It is a captive life,
a timid life, a life where mere survival
is the choice at any price because beyond it there is nothing,
nothing at all. And therefore friendship, honor, justice,
even love, fall into second place, if necessary
will have to be abandoned in order to evade
the end of everything.

I once heard from a fisherman that you don't need
a top for a crab trap, because the moment that one captive
tries to climb toward the top, the others always
claw it down again. Such is life
when death, and its avoidance, is the all-consuming master.
So that, if one lives this way, one eventually finds oneself
with a hammer in one's hand and nails, crucifying others
in order to escape the cross oneself.

What, then, of those who serve the powers of life,
who seek in freedom and in faith to trust themselves
to life, give themselves in service, share all they have
with those less fortunate?
You lived this life, Lord Jesus,
as you walked the land of Palestine,
teaching, healing, blessing all you met until you met with
treachery, betrayal, and the cross.

Then what, pray tell me, is the difference here?
Why should I live for life, rather than in fear of death,
if I ultimately wind up at the cross in either case?
Is it better to be the victim than to be the executioner?

Is it preferable to pound in the nails rather than
to know them in one's own tender flesh? Is this all, at best,
a Hobson's choice, no choice at all, since both paths end up
in the same old place, the six-foot drop,
"ashes to ashes, dust to dust"?

If your story ended on Good Friday, Lord,
then this would be the only valid conclusion.
But on Easter Day the tomb was empty,
the women all came running with their news.
And Peter, John, the two who journeyed to Emmaus,
those fishers on the shore,
Paul on the Damascus road,
echoed their cry, "The Lord is risen indeed!"
In this the faith was born: not the bleak guilt and sorrow
of Golgotha, but the history-shattering affirmation
of the Easter garden. And here the difference lies:
that life lived openly and free has triumphed over
death and all death's powers; that the heart of this
whole universe has revealed itself once and for all as love,
endless compassion, a vast and cosmic tenderness
for me and all of this creation.

Two masters, then: death, of course, and life.
Let me choose life, Lord God, not only with my lips,
my prayers tonight, but with every living atom of my being.
I ask it through the risen Christ.
                         Amen.

DAY TWENTY-NINE
Anxiety
Matthew 6:25–32

Therefore I tell you, do not be anxious about your life, what you shall eat or what you shall drink, nor about your body, what you shall put on.

MORNING

This saying, "Do not be anxious," recalls me to
a rainy, chilly Monday afternoon in Edinburgh. I was home
in Scotland on a visit to my family, and toward the end of a day
of typically Scottish weather—tantalizing glimpses of the sun
alternating with the windblown, North Sea rain—I was
hurrying across North Bridge, heading for the first bus
that would take me home to a warm fire,
a dry change of clothes.
Just as I reached the middle of the bridge,
right opposite that marvelous old heroic statue
to the Scottish soldiers killed in the Boer War, the sun
broke through once more, and behold! a rainbow,
in all its springtime colors, arching full across that symbol
of past sacrifice, death, and glory.

It was drizzling still a bit, and my impulse
was to hurry on with the rest of the crowd. But something
in that scene called out to me. I stopped and, for want
of an excuse, pulled out my pocket camera to take a photograph.
The throng pressed by: pedestrians in their usual city scramble,
double-decker buses with the passengers looking down,
I'm sure, at this crazy tourist standing in the rain.
Then I too joined the crowd again;
and it was only later, on reflection with that snapshot,
that I realized all I had seen.

That rainbow, Lord, took in so much.
It began beyond the Calton Hill, a fine, imposing landmark
on which stand several buildings of some note and notoriety.
There is another war memorial, "Edinburgh's Folly,"
people call it, because the citizens began
to build it after the Battle of Waterloo—a replica
of the Parthenon—and then ran out of funds.
Yet today it stands for all the world just like
that noble Grecian ruin. Nearby stands the Calton Jail,
where convicted malefactors, long ago, eked out
what still remained to them of wretched life.
There is a famous cemetery there, with various illustrious
remains. There is the old Observatory, where scientists
once sought to map the heavens. The Royal High School lies
to one side, one of Scotland's finest educational institutions.
There are monuments there to Burns, Nelson,
even Abraham Lincoln.
And then the rainbow leaped across and ended just between
the royal palace, Holyrood, and Arthur's Seat—
the massive old extinct volcano which dominates
the city to the south.

What a span that was! including, representing there
beneath its arch so much of human wisdom, human folly:
war and grief, youth and poetry, failure and hope,
learning, royalty, and mortality.
There was a sign for me in that bright arch
embracing all our enterprises, dreams, and failures
within its graceful loveliness. For the rainbow is more
than a mere illustration of refraction, of the effect of light
on raindrops. It speaks, has spoken since the world began,
of trust, trust in you, Lord God;
a reminder of your covenant of grace.
Yet the crowds hurried past unseeing, unheeding,
preoccupied with all the daily doings of this city
called the world. They scurried by as I so often do.
No time to heed the message of the rainbow. No time to read
the signals of the lilies that neither toil nor spin,
yet know much more of glory than my poor, frantic soul
can ever comprehend, aspire to.

Let me take time this day, Lord God.
Alert my inner eye, my quiet ear, that I may yet
perceive the secret of the stars, the birds, the oceans.
Teach me to be, and not always to do. And let my being
rest in you, my Rock and my Redeemer.

                                                    Amen.

EVENING

I saw another rainbow once
I never have forgotten, Lord.
I was flying, transatlantic, on the old Icelandic Airlines
when my plane, traversing banks of cloud, was caught
and held a moment by a shaft of piercing sunlight.
There below on the cloud face
was a perfect circled rainbow.

Not only that, but at the center of that spectrum
was a cross, formed by the shadow of that old
propeller-driven airplane. The circled rainbow and the cross.
That ancient sign of yours—from Noah's time—
Lord God, made perfect now, made whole, complete,
around the emblem of Christ's death
for me, for all.

I live an anxious life
much of the time, O God; live it in
what has been called the "Age of Anxiety."
There are the kids to get through school and college,
the roof, the car that needs repair, the nagging backache
that wakes me in the night to questions about health,
finances, future. And somewhere, in behind all these,
there is the Bomb and all it represents.

So that your gift to me of life
is all too often taken up, consumed
in fearful dread.

Lord, as that rainbow centered on the cross
illuminates my memory, so let the truth it represents
shed light and peace upon my soul this night.
In that sign of loving sacrifice
held at the heart of all the glory of creation
may I find a sign to guide me through the clouds
of trepidation and concern, to lead me home to you,
in faith, through Jesus Christ, my Shepherd
and my Guide.
    Amen.

DAY THIRTY
Seeking the Kingdom
Matthew 6:33–34

But seek first his kingdom and his righteousness, and all these things shall be yours as well

MORNING

I recently reviewed my life insurance, Lord,
made some adjustments because they told me this was
the prudent thing to do, after all, on reaching the
advancing age of fifty. Yet you admonish me to take no thought
for the morrow, to live on simple trust just like the birds
of the air, the flowers of the field.
Did you mean us all to be Franciscans, Jesus,
to live from day to day, from hand to mouth?
If so, it would not work; for even the Franciscans
needed someone else to beg from, were dependent
on the Christian charity of others.

The Greek here, so they tell me,
forbids *"anxious* thought," pernicious worry;
not a sensible provision to take care of realistic future needs.
Your concern is with the tendency for reasonable worries
to become swiftly unreasonable, to feed upon themselves,
to escalate, expand till they take over
at the center of a life and thus displace what should be there:
the love of God, the seeking of God's kingdom.

You suggest, or so I read these words,
that if my life is focused where it ought to be,
if my first priority is always to seek out and do
the Father's will, then thoughts, plans,

provisions for the future, will naturally resume
their proper, balanced, healthy role—and all within
the framework of a quiet trust.

The kingdom: you have shown it to me
in countless actions, stories, parables;
by your whole life. Help me, this day, to seek it
where the lost is found, the broken mended,
the hungry fed, the grieving comforted. Reveal, again,
your kingdom to me in wedding feasts and funerals,
in marketplaces, justice halls, and fishing boats.
Unveil within the everyday the sacrament
of life in all its vibrant, hopeful power.
And lead me, in that power, to grasp your kingdom
in the hands and hearts of everyone I meet today.

                                             Amen.

EVENING

"One day at a time":
this saying, Lord, has been adopted
as a slogan by so many cancer patients,
so many persons whose day-to-day routine has been
abruptly interrupted by a reality shared by all your children—
if unacknowledged, for the most part—the reality of death.

Yet the impact of this message must not be reserved
for those whose sights have been suddenly
and drastically lowered, whose life expectancy
is fearfully reduced at one fell swoop.
"One day at a time" is the basic precondition
of every human life, and it is essential for sanity
to admit this to oneself. This harsh—at first—

yet healing truth provides protection against crippling worry
that can dominate and crush if not controlled;
that can transform life from a joyful, free adventure
to a fearful tiptoed traverse of a minefield.

Life lived one day at a time
receives each day as it is given,
attempts to find in it, draw out from it,
its quotient share of happiness and pain,
of tenderness and insight, work and play, both
duty and delight. It treats each day as if it were the last—
as well it might be—and therefore carries into it
no dreary, unforgiven burdens from the past,
and leaves undone, unsaid, no word or act
of tenderness and kindness.

Life lived one day at a time puts
all our eggs into one basket—today—
and makes of them a splendid, fragrant,
taste-exploding omelet, to munch on, family style.
Then sets the basket out again in trust
the hens will lay again tomorrow.

Forgive, O Lord, my domineering little worries,
fears, forebodings, and help me live the freedom that springs
from trusting the future to your hands: your creating,
healing, grace-revealing hands.
                                        Amen.

DAY THIRTY-ONE
On Judging
Matthew 7:1-5

Judge not, that you be not judged. For with the judgment you pronounce you will be judged, and the measure you give will be the measure you get.

MORNING

I just heard on the news of a teenager
sent to jail for driving a car. He was on parole, Lord,
forbidden to drive because, three years ago, he had run down
a student nurse: killed her outright while drag racing
along a city street. On the same news
I heard about savage attacks upon defenseless civilians
in Lebanon, about high-level corporate schemes
to defraud the government, about drug dealers caught
in a scam, about corrupt police and public officials.

And I judged, Lord God. In my mind I became
judge and jury, formulated verdicts,
passed down sentences.

My daughter asks if she can stay out late for Senior Prom.
A colleague calls, inquires if he should make a deal or just
sit tight. There's an offer in the mail, a way
to get rich quick, to borrow easy money. A decision
must be made whether to fire or rehire.
And I am judging once again. Indeed, the more
I look at daily life, the more I realize:
I do an awful lot of judging.

You tell me, bluntly, not to judge, Lord Jesus.
"Judge not, that you be not judged." How am I to

reconcile these words of yours with this simple mental act
so much a part of my everyday existence?
The whole thing gets even more confused, Lord,
when I note in this same Sermon on the Mount
your exhortation to "Beware of false prophets,
who come to you in sheep's clothing but inwardly
are ravenous wolves." Is this not judging? And if so,
how am I to reconcile these two opposing teachings
within some fifteen verses?

Judging, of course, can mean so many things:
all the way from evaluating the relative merits
of wines, works of art, automobiles to declaring someone
must be put to death in the electric chair.
Might it, then, be possible to draw some fine distinctions;
to separate out judgment of mere things from that of persons?

What you advocate here, Lord, it seems to me,
is not so much the suspension of the entire critical
faculty; rather, it is concern with the condemning aspect—
that self-righteous, finger-pointing censoriousness
which so eagerly creeps in. As a believer
in a certain understanding of the world
I cannot simply smile, hold my peace, and pretend
that everything in the garden is just rosy.
I have to speak my mind, my faith, on what is right
and wrong, true and false. But I do not have—
and this is where the tricky part comes in—
I am not thereby licensed to condemn any and all who
differ with me.

Lord God, as I judge this day—and judge I must—
deliver me from all impulse to self-righteous condemnation.
Grant me clear discernment,
sympathy with my fellow human beings,
and the spirit of forgiveness. In Christ, my Lord.
                                                  Amen.

EVENING

The record of your church on this commandment,
"Judge not, that you be not judged," is one of miserable failure,
Lord. The evidences of that failure lie all across the globe
in the vast multiplicity of sects, confessions,
groupings, denominations: all of them believing,
or having believed at one time, that they were in the right,
and all the rest were wrong.

So it has been that rather than continue
to debate, dispute, converse, confer, reason, argue—
whatever—with fellow believers, Christians
for the most part have chosen to condemn:
have denounced all those who could not see exactly eye-to-eye
with them as heretics and worse; have leaped to judgment
rather than agree to differ amicably and in mutual respect.

There must, of course, be differences at times.
Fellow Christians may, in the opinion of others,
go astray, fall into error on some point or another.
And that error may be pointed out, within the proper context;
can be debated, studied, resolved, corrected, even,
if such a thing be possible. But whether possible or not,
that error cannot qualify the rest to judge,
condemn, cast out from fellowship.
Such judgments, I believe, belong to you, Lord Christ,
and you did not drive even Judas from your table.
To judge the sin, then, but not the sinner:
that is how I comprehend your teaching here, Lord.
And it gets very difficult at times, especially when the sin
is of the magnitude of a holocaust, or of a crucifixion.
But whoever said this Sermon on the Mount was simple,
easy to apply?

Lord, make me so conscious of your grace,
amazing grace to me, that I may never look again with scorn
or hateful condemnation on my fellow human beings.
Show me how I can abhor sin, injustice, evil,
yet still extend to others the same forgiveness
that I would ask for myself: that forgiveness
you have won for all God's people, Lord.
                                        Amen.

DAY THIRTY-TWO
The Holy
Matthew 7:6

Do not give dogs what is holy; and do not throw your pearls before swine, lest they trample them under foot and turn to attack you.

MORNING

This saying, Lord, is a troublesome one.
Like your rebuke of that poor Canaanite woman
who came to you for healing for her child
and you told her you would not
"throw the children's bread to the dogs."
There is a strangeness here, a seeming tone of intolerance
that does not fit the rest of your teachings.
Who or what did you mean to refer to here
as the dogs, or as the swine? Having just told me not to judge,
are you now changing all that: saying that I can call people
by such names as these after all; telling me to deny
to them the message of the kingdom?

This is, in fact, one of those passages
with which I need to wrestle long and hard.
Might it be that in this saying you are seeking
to redress the balance of your teaching about judgment?
Could you, perhaps, be telling me that while I can
condemn no other person, yet certain lesser judgments
are still appropriate, if not required?

One would not, for example, approach
an avowed atheist and a committed Christian
of a different persuasion from your own in precisely
the same way. In terms of holy things, whereas one might

112

enjoy a meal with the first, engage in lively conversation,
debate across the table as one human being exchanging
views with another, one would not invite this skeptic
to the table of the Lord. That sacramental mystery has been
reserved, from the beginning, to believers or,
at least, to all who would seek life in Christ,
who come in humble faith, seeking grace alone, not answers,
proofs, or disputations. Yet with a fellow Christian,
even of a different group, one might share in
the Lord's Supper. Are you, then, calling here
less for judgment than for a certain wise discernment?

Or again, are you warning me, Lord,
that in the "selling" of your gospel I can make it
all too cheap, too readily available, too watered-down
to meet the common taste? Are there, for example,
ways in which folk market Christianity nowadays
that present it more as dog food, pig swill, than as
the pearl of great price, the holy,
awe-inspiring Word of God?

I cannot despise my fellow human beings
in such scathing terms as these, Lord Christ.
You, yourself, have already warned against it most severely.
Therefore guide me as I seek to understand this difficult word,
and let me grow in wisdom and compassion.

Amen.

EVENING

Whereas I am not at all sure just what
you mean by "dogs" or "swine" in this verse, Lord,
I am convinced of the reality of the holy.
There are places, there are times, which are set apart
for you, Lord God. And the sacredness they gather
has a power that cannot be denied.

People—still today—call a church a "house of God."
And although there are many who would say
they don't believe in it, and though many who do believe
are convinced that you are everywhere revealed,
that no spot on earth can be a stranger to your holy
presence; still, on entering your house,
there are few who do not bow the head,
remove the hat, and hush the voice.

There is a basic sense of reverence,
a fundamental aura of the holy, Lord, that cannot
be ignored without great effort or great ignorance.
I have tasted this experience in Europe: in the busy,
secular streets of a great city, when the bells
of some cathedral, or a tiny parish church, peal forth
across the rooftops, waken sleeping dogs and pigeons,
waken sleeping souls, and cause all eyes to lift
above the sidewalks, even to glance, somewhat furtively,
toward heaven.

Such timely calls to prayer and contemplation,
such shrines wherein the soul finds majesty and marvel,
rest and sustenance, such fragments of your presence
as you have vouchsafed to us your wandering children,
are truly sacred: must not be defamed or spat upon,
neglected. It is to this reverent keeping, guarding,
preserving that this verse calls me tonight.

Continue, Lord, to bless my life
with revelations, manifestations of the holy
in the midst of time and space. And when, and as,
I know your nearer presence, may there be within me
nothing that profanes or desecrates the wonder
and the glory of it all.
                    Amen.

DAY THIRTY-THREE
Great Expectations
Matthew 7:7–11

Ask, and it will be given you; seek, and you will find; knock, and it will be opened to you. For every one who asks receives, every one who seeks finds, and to every one who knocks it will be opened.

MORNING

A blank check.
That is what this word of yours
seems to be promising here, Lord . . . a blank check.
Not only that, but a blank check drawn on God!

I received a blank check once. We were in Maine,
staying at our vacation cottage, and needed some lumber
and supplies for improvements I was planning to the place.
Before we set off on the boat for the mainland,
we were talking the plans over with a friend—
an island carpenter—getting the benefit of his free advice
on what to buy and where to go to buy it. At some point
I must have said I wasn't sure we had enough money
to afford everything we contemplated because,
when we left his house, my friend drew me aside
and quietly pushed into my pocket a blank check
all signed and ready to be drawn on his account.
I was totally surprised and very touched he trusted me
that much. As it turned out, we didn't need the extra funds.
But to this day, I still tease him about how, someday,
I will cash it in and leave him in deep trouble.

Blank checks are tricky things to handle.
When you said, "Ask, and you will receive," Lord,
did you really mean that all I have to do is let God know

I want something and God will then deliver . . . guaranteed?
That is certainly what it sounds like.

There are preachers on TV who talk this way. They claim
that if I will only pray hard enough, believe hard enough,
and give hard enough (sending them a fat donation in the mail),
God will supply me with whatever it is I ask for.
They make an awful lot of money preaching that way, so I guess
at least their prayers are answered. But I'm not so sure
exactly who they're praying to. I'm not at all convinced
this is the way you work with me, Lord God.

If you really granted all my prayers just as
I asked them, sheer chaos would almost certainly result.
Indeed, I can imagine a hilarious TV or movie script
entitled "The Man Whose Prayers Were Answered."

The ancient Greeks knew this. They told the story of Aurora—
goddess of the dawn—and her love for a young mortal
named Tithonus. Aurora pled with Zeus, king of gods,
that her lover be allowed to live forever. Her prayer
was granted . . . except that she forgot to ask that he
remain forever young. The gift became a curse
as Tithonus grew older, ever older, yet could never die.

I thank you, Lord, that you have not responded
to my prayers by granting me exactly what I ask for.
I thank you that your wisdom overrules my foolishness,
your love corrects my shallow and shortsighted human desires.
So let that wisdom and that love guide me today;
and thus may all my living be a prayer of praise to you.

Amen.

EVENING

You answer all my prayers, Lord.
Of that I am persuaded; but you do not always answer them
by granting me whatever I request.

One day when I was nine or ten years old
I got caught smoking a cigarette in the toilets
behind the church. There were six of us, Boy Scouts,
in a circle passing the awful thing around and, of course,
just at my turn, the scoutmaster walked in and caught us all.

I prayed, Lord, did I ever pray! I prayed that,
whatever that scoutmaster did, he would not tell my father.
He told him. My prayers went unanswered, or so I thought.
And yet, I've never smoked another cigarette;
and my dad and I
had such a talk that day—man-to-man, not angry—
that I have never yet forgotten it,
and don't suppose I ever will. Was my prayer, then,
not answered? Or was it answered in a different, far better way
than I could ever have wished for, prayed for?

I recall your prayer, Lord Jesus Christ, your prayer
one lonely night in a Garden in the city of Jerusalem.
You were afraid; knowing what you knew of all that lay ahead
on the next day. You were frightened, just as I too
would have been. And that fear of yours does not disturb me;
rather, it brings you closer to me. You prayed then
to your Father, God, that you would not have to carry through
your mission to the end, that the "bitter cup" could
pass you by—your life be spared.
Yet, in the end, you closed your prayer with these words,
"Not my will, but thine, be done"; "Not what I want, Father,
but whatever you in wisdom and in love know has to be."

Had you been granted what you asked for in that Garden, Lord,
there would have been no Good Friday; that other garden scene
beside the empty tomb could never have occurred.
Thank God it was not so! Thank you, Lord,
that not your will but God's was done, and I today
can pray this prayer with freedom and in hope.

In that freedom and that hope I lay me down to rest.
Hear these my evening prayers, my personal requests,
my committing of my loved ones to your keeping, and answer,
not exactly as I ask, but according to your vision
of my life and of its purpose from this night
into eternity.

       Amen.

DAY THIRTY-FOUR
The Golden Rule
Matthew 7:12

So whatever you wish that others would do to you, do so to them; for this is the law and the prophets.

MORNING

As I sat meditating in my study one recent morning—
I was preparing for a sermon on this text
"Do as you would be done by"—I was interrupted
and then intrigued by a series of sharp cries
coming from somewhere just outside the study window.
I crossed the room to investigate and there, on the corner
of the college playing field below, I watched
another religious exercise taking place.
Three youngsters, somewhere between ten and fifteen years,
two boys and a little girl—her hair in bunches—
and all clad in gleaming white with colored sashes round
their waists, moved, under the tutelage of two adult instructors,
through the ritualized aggression of karate.
First they advanced together as a group, almost
a graceful corps de ballet, but with clenched fists, set jaws,
kicking high their feet in sharp, potentially lethal jabs
and letting out intimidating yells in unison.
Next they turned their stylized skills upon each other;
obviously expert at an early age in what they call
"the martial arts"—the artistry, in other words,
of hurting, maiming, killing.
I shuddered to think of tangling with such children
in Sunday school, especially if they chose to disagree
with whatever I was teaching; then turned back

to the desk and to this Golden Rule, "So whatever you wish
that others would do to you, do so to them."

There is an irony here, Lord, a tragic irony:
two worlds existing side by side. Inside the study,
the high ideal, the hope, promise, possibility of humankind;
out there, in brilliant sunshine, on the green grass of spring,
the harsh reality of fear, self-defense, pain, and death.
Just what connection is there . . . is there possible
between these two contrasting worlds, Lord?
What good does it do for preachers to climb into
their pulpits, Sunday after Sunday, to proclaim this
Golden Rule, if the rest of the world, the rest of the week,
is muttering, "Do unto others before they do unto you"
and perfecting their karate chops?

Is this Golden Rule just that: a lovely phrase,
an elegant idea, a piece of timeless inspiration that should
be set in golden letters above the lintels of our temples
and then forgotten while we go on to plan our Star Wars,
our preemptive nuclear strikes?

Lord, let me take this Golden Rule, this near cliché
of popular morality, and try to live it for one day
in this angry and defensive world. In each encounter
may this word ring in my ears and echo in my deeds,
"Do as you would be done by." Strengthen me where I succeed.
Support and comfort, cleanse me where I fail,
and all in Jesus' name.
                              Amen.

EVENING

This rule of yours, Lord Jesus,
is known and respected, admired throughout the entire
human family. In every literature and language,
in almost every culture and religion, its simple,
basic message has been echoed and reechoed. Why, then,
is it so seldom practiced, so rarely put into action
in the daily wear and tear of relationships?

It is not, after all, a very lofty, super-high ideal.
The Golden Rule demands no necessary sacrifice, no noble,
idealistic self-surrender. It appeals more to
a simple reciprocity, a kind of tit for tat
lived in reverse. Far from one-sided altrusim,
this might even be described as the most logical expression
of enlightened self-interest, teaching that the best way
to achieve a pleasant and harmonious life is to treat others
in this way, so they will do the same to you.
An implicit kind of bargain, social contract, lies beneath,
not all that far from "I'll scratch your back, you'll
scratch mine." Yet for all its common sense,
its logical simplicity, it has seldom been
successfully lived out.

One kind of complication might arise from the fact
that not everyone desires to be treated quite the same.
Individuals may be so different, Lord—
each one unique as you created them—
that to treat them all exactly as I would have them all
treat me might create as many problems as it solved.
For example, to be gentle to a masochist
could be a subtle form of Inquisition.

Perhaps the major drawback here lies in the observation
that this rule, if perfectly applied, would bring about equality,
would make all persons' rights the same, entitled to
identical consideration and respect. While I may claim
to believe in such equality, Father, in my inner self
I have not been persuaded. Deep inside I am convinced
that I am special, above the masses, deserving of
a little something extra here and there—and mostly here.
Or even worse, I am persuaded that I am actually inferior
and that if I were to open up, treat others

in the way that I deserve, then I would end up
even more of a loser than I am right now.

Deliver me from all such complications, Lord.
Humble my pride. Help me accept myself as your beloved child.
Root me firm and deep within the family that knows you as
"our Father," never only "my Father." Set me on a level
with every other sinner for whom your Son died.
And reveal to me the wonder and the privilege
of such a chosen status.

So, seeing others as I see myself, might I extend to them
the care and the concern that, all too often, I reserve
for myself. So may your Golden Rule inform,
instruct, and even yet redeem my days.

Amen.

DAY THIRTY-FIVE
The Straight and Narrow
Matthew 7:13–14

Enter by the narrow gate; for the gate is wide and the way is easy, that leads to destruction, and those who enter by it are many.

MORNING

Decision is what you are after here, Lord.
You have more or less completed, at this point,
the content of your teachings: spelled out your portrait
of the believer in the Beatitudes; redefined the law
from its solely external application toward the issues
of internal motivation; taught about praying,
fasting, giving alms; issued severe warnings about judging
and the like; and here, as I see it, you begin
to drive your message home with a call for decision.

I'm not too comfortable with this, however,
this demand for a clear-cut choice between the narrow
and the broad. Aren't you getting a bit too dramatic,
a bit too evangelical, Lord? Couldn't I take some time,
a couple of weeks, perhaps, or months,
to think things over calmly? Is this not all a bit
high-pressured, a touch manipulative, to insist
that I decide right here, right now?

Yet life, you tell me, does not work that way.
Life is a process of choices, forks in the road,
where decisions must be made and there are no time-outs.
As one of those slogans from the sixties reminds me,
"Not to decide is to decide." If I do not choose

the narrow way, I will be swept along with
the crowd into the broad.

On the other hand, Lord, too much can be made
of this decisiveness; as if it were a once-for-all-time
sort of thing. I know far too many Christians who can tell
the precise date, hour, minute of their "conversion":
but could not even guess the last time they acted out their faith
in a decision in their work, their home, their community.

As I see life, Lord God, it is a road with many intersections,
each one of which presents me with the choice
to either live my faith or deny it, to trust in you
or trust in my own self. There is a valid, vital sense
in which the decisions that I face each day,
in my personal relationships, in the struggle for integrity
and responsibility on the job, in my attitudes and actions
on the major public issues: war and peace, hunger,
abortion, human rights . . . in these choices
I am becoming, or failing to become, a Christian.
And in them I define myself far more clearly than
by any words I speak, any button I pin on my lapel.

As I arise this day, O God, direct my feet to the strait gate,
toward the narrow way. Let me walk into the world,
not with a yawn, a groan, a grudge deep inside,
but with praise and true thanksgiving
on my lips and in my heart.
Amen.

EVENING

Nobody wants to be narrow nowadays.
This is not at all a popular choice, Lord.
The thing is to be broad, broad-minded, tolerant,
generous to a fault. And, at its best, I know that this
can be a very positive, appealing characteristic.
Yet it can also lead to a vast and meaningless zero.

Breadth without depth means shallowness in my experience;
and there is a danger that, in accepting everything, I wind up
believing nothing. Could it be, Lord, that much of my
own tolerance is just another name for indifference?

The narrowness you call for here, Lord Christ,
need not be, surely, a self-righteous narrowness
that would exclude all those who differ. Rather, I should
imagine a narrowness that focuses like a lens, that sharpens,
concentrates the vision; a narrowness that can clarify,
commit a life to goals that it believes worth living for.

People, after all, are willing to give up
all sorts of things. It's quite acceptable to narrow in,
focus down, and sacrifice in order to become, say,
a concert violinist or a surgeon, a shortstop in
the major leagues. But to ask the same in order to be like you,
Lord Christ, to live toward the goals you taught, to taste
abundant life, would be seen by many as
some kind of weird fanaticism.

To be a Christian demands this kind of dedication.
It is no easy thing—just like falling off a log.
Those profit-seeking preachers, who will guarantee to solve
all problems, cure all ailments, bring about success
in worldly terms, are not preaching the same gospel
that you preached, Jesus Lord.
Nothing in life worth having seems to be attained
without effort and sacrifice. How much more, then,
the greatest thing, the very secret of life itself?

A year and more ago I stood in Bethlehem Square,
outside the massive Church of the Nativity. Facing me,
the only entrance to that ancient shrine, was
a low and narrow doorway: an opening that had, it seemed,

been sized down in stages over the centuries
from a grand, magnificent archway into a shadowed aperture
we had to enter one by one and with heads deeply bowed.
Inside was all the splendor of centuries of piety
and holiness—the very spot where God's life
became flesh like mine. But I had to enter
by that tiny door.

So with the faith you present here. The gate
may be strait, the way narrow, but the life to which it leads
is radiant, full, forever. Grant me humility to enter
by that lowly door, Lord, and trust to walk
the narrow way with you.
                    Amen.

DAY THIRTY-SIX
By Their Fruits
Matthew 7:15–20

Beware of false prophets, who come to you in sheep's clothing but inwardly are ravenous wolves. You will know them by their fruits.

MORNING

For a message that seems so simple,
"You will know them by their fruits," these verses
bear the potential for great problems in the church. It would
be all too easy, Lord, to read and then proceed to carry out
what one scholar calls "a fruit inspection."
In other words, to go about examining other Christians,
other churches, on the basis of this text: judging,
and even possibly condemning them.
This cannot be your intention, Lord.
In view of your strict teaching against judgment,
there is no way to use these verses as a hunting permit
against fellow believers.

In fact, properly understood, this saying might support
a deeper tolerance for others. So long as we have focused
on beliefs, we Christians have historically had trouble
recognizing and respecting one another.
It has been just as if you taught us,
"By their creeds, confessions, doctrines,
you shall know them." If we could focus on the fruits,
evaluate the faith of fellow Christians, not on the basis
of their doctrine of the sacraments alone, but rather
on the evidence we see of Christian love,
the hungry children fed,

the homeless housed, the captives of all kinds set free,
then our ecumenical relations might find new impetus.

When John the Baptist, Lord, from jail,
sent followers to ask about your mission, your identity,
you presented to them no lengthy theological treatise;
simply told them to tell John all that they had seen and heard:

> The blind receive their sight and the lame walk,
> lepers are cleansed and the deaf hear,
> and the dead are raised up,
> and the poor have good news preached to them.

It has happened like this on the mission field
when, in face of such enormous need, there was no time
for all the petty prejudice, the bickering and rivalry of
the home front. Why, then, can the church not see
about its very doors, in this secular, fragmented,
and increasingly faithless society, an equally urgent need
for the living fruits of Christian faith
in the form of compassion, healing, tenderness, and hope?
Only such a vision can draw true Christians together.
Only such a practical approach can bring back
the disillusioned to the family of faith.

Teach me, Lord God, to recognize that family,
my family, wherever I can see the ripe fruits
of your Holy Spirit. And grant that, by your grace,
others too may find such fruits in me.

Amen.

EVENING

This teaching about fruits, Lord Christ,
is too easily dealt with if I use it only to
evaluate the faith of others. It speaks to and asks
questions of my faith also.

This very act of prayer, for one thing—the entire experience,
in fact, of Christian worship—is interrogated by these words.
At its best, worship is the very core of Christian life,
the dynamo from which I draw the spark to power
every other aspect of discipleship and service.
But prayer and worship, at their worst, can become,
not a spark, but a substitute for action, Lord.
There is for me, in worship, both the aesthetic and the ethic,
both beauty there and duty. The two are indispensable.
But the beauty, all alone, can be seductive.
I can be quickly swept away by the grandeur of an anthem,
the stateliness of holy, ancient language, the rich textures
of stained glass, carved wood and stone, and forget
that all these elements lead and must lead to
that holiest of moments when your voice, Lord, calls,
"Whom shall I send?" And I respond in humble,
willing obedience, "Here am I, Lord. Send me."
Worship must bear fruit, and prayer too,
or it is nothing but idolatry, the adoration
of sheer emptiness.

Lord, I hear your warning in this teaching.
I realize that I fall short: that, all too often, the fruit
I bear is meager, minute, bitter to the taste.
Yet you remind me, also, that I am not the best judge of myself,
my life and witness; that you can and still do use me
in ways I cannot discern, perhaps will never know about.
So grant that, by your grace, I might bring forth
good fruit, rich and ripe and full of seeded
promise for the future.
                    Amen.

DAY THIRTY-SEVEN
Lord, Lord
Matthew 7:21–23

Not every one who says to me, "Lord, Lord," shall enter the kingdom of heaven, but those who do the will of my Father who is in heaven.

MORNING

"Ever'body talkin' 'bout heaven ain't a-goin' there,"
so goes that great old spiritual. And yet, of all those
who have sung its words, of all those who have preached upon
this text—"Not every one who says to me, 'Lord, Lord' "—
I wonder how many have believed it of themselves,
have actually accepted its message that, for all their singing,
all their preaching, all their testimony to the faith,
they may never see the kingdom.

Religious busywork can be just as sure a road to hell
as any of the other, much more lurid avenues.
Your church, Lord Christ, and all its multiple activities,
demands, responsibilities, has its own quite deadly way
of standing square between Christians
and their calling, between believers
and their mission in the world.

It is so easy, Lord, so satisfying,
to get caught up in all the meetings and the functions,
the fellowship and study groups and prayer circles.
People gain from all of this a sense that they
truly are "about their Father's business"; that they
are giving of themselves in pure and sacrificial service.
When so much of what they do can merely be the keeping
of wheels spinning in the air: the support of an institution

130

that can be just as sinful, as self-centered
and self-satisfied as any of its members.

The clergy, Father, are especially suspect
in this area. This has to be an occupational hazard
for such Christians, Lord: identifying everything they do
as "in the service of the kingdom"; seeing themselves
as "full-time servants of the Lord." When most of what
even the best of them achieve is, in truth,
much more mixed, both in motivation and in result.

Help me, Lord, to sift the good grain from the chaff
in what I call my Christian service. Make me honest with myself
to discern when I am serving you and when I am self-serving.
Make clear to me each time I am engaged in semi-urgent,
semi-needful work that keeps me from the crucial tasks you have
for me to accomplish. Teach me to appreciate
the church for all it is and can be—a company who join
in acts of mystery, praise, and grace, a fellowship
of true support and comfort, growth and shared endeavor.
But protect me from making it a substitute for the kingdom.
Guide me, this day, to know and do the Father's will.
So may I cry, "Lord, Lord," in honest, living faith.
Amen.

EVENING

The Day of Judgment—"On that day . . ."—
is not a concept people talk about much anymore, Lord,
outside of hymns and awkward scripture passages like this one.
The whole idea of an afterlife, of some existence
beyond death, seems generally suspect in these times,
associated with the fringe religious groups,
the cults, or pop psychology.

Yet throughout all the history of humankind,
back to the most primitive remains, artifacts, burial customs,
such a belief has played a vital role in comprehending
what this gift of life is all about.

Sometimes, Lord, the naked arrogance
of my own generation fills me with as much embarrassment
as astonishment. This "modern age" is so convinced
that it alone has unlocked all the secrets,
or will do so very soon. It firmly believes
as an essential tenet of its self-esteem that every era
until now was trapped in gloomy ignorance, dark superstition.
The "wisdom of the ages" has become a meaningless expression.

That wisdom is still there, nevertheless,
to be listened to by all who would be wise. And that wisdom,
from all ages and all cultures, tells me there will be
a day of reckoning, tells me you are not deceived
by pious prattle, holy language as a smoke screen,
tells me you will weigh my life, my actions
and inactions in the balances.

Lord, "on that day," may I stand fast,
not on any merit of my own, but in your grace, O Christ.
Yet may I also know at least some growth in faith,
some progress in discipleship, some true obedience in love
that I may offer them, not for my salvation,
but in humble gratitude and praise.
                                        Amen.

132

DAY THIRTY-EIGHT
Foundations
Matthew 7:24–27

Every one then who hears these words of mine and does them will be like someone wise enough to build a house upon the rock.

MORNING

Two ways you set before me, Lord, the narrow
and the broad. Two trees, a sound tree bearing good fruit,
a bad tree bearing evil. And now I see two houses,
one on sand, the other firm on rock.

There is so much sand to build on; and it is so very tempting,
so easy just to lay the four-by-fours along the ground, maybe even
pound them in as far and as deep as they will penetrate,
then go ahead and build a frame around them.
Life, the way we live it nowadays, encourages,
almost compels us toward, this attitude.
There is so much to be done,
so much to see and taste, experience. And it is all set
before folk at such an early age that who has time
to dig foundations anymore, to prepare for winter storms
up ahead? After all, the way this world is headed,
who knows if we will make it through till winter?

I saw some photographs in a news magazine some months ago,
right in between the latest scenes of carnage from Beirut
and the painted, masklike faces of the latest
millionaire rock idols. They were aerial shots
of real estate along the beaches: high-rise condos in Miami,
luxury houses crammed along the narrowest of causeways,
spits of sand, no more, with ocean waves on either side.

And the whole scene hung together: violence and bloodshed
on the one hand, false gods and banality on the other,
and in between a host of Babel towers,
reaching for heavenly happiness, striving to exist like gods,
with their feet sunk in the shifting sands that doom them.

Why not? Why not take a chance?
Maybe I'll be lucky. Maybe the dice of life will roll
just right, and there will be no winter storm to face—
just sunshine and high living all the way
until the end. It happens, after all.
Folk make it like that every day.
Why couldn't it be me?

What is it that they make it to . . . to death?
Is that the goal, to make it somehow through to death,
unscathed? Is that what I am here for, what people
all around me are settling for today? Then they are building
upon sand . . . shifting sand. Just like that fool
in the parable, Lord, I hear these words—the Sermon
on the Mount—I admire them, respect them, maybe even study,
analyze, and pray about them, but I do not live them.
And the sand is rising all the time, is rising
past my ankles, almost to my knees.

Lord, teach me about rock and sand. Set my life,
this day, upon the firm foundation you have laid,
laid by the wood and nails you bore on Calvary,
O Master Carpenter. Then build in me
and through me your kingdom, Lord.

                                        Amen.

EVENING

Which will it be? you ask me tonight, Lord.
Will it be rock or will it be sand? Will I choose
comfort and convenience, the carefree easy life, or can I
opt for caring, concern, compassion, community, the cross?

The rock I know. I have felt it firm beneath my feet
in this holy book, these words of yours I have considered now
for almost forty days, this act of prayer acknowledging
your presence, your judgment, your forgiving grace.
The rock is here. It has been shown to me,
set before me now amid the sinking sands of time.

Will I set my feet upon its firmness?
It is not soft, warm, yielding, easy like the sand.
It feels rough, hard, gritty, maybe a little cold and chill.
But it will stand forever, yes, through all
the winter storms and on into eternal sunlight,
the sunlight of your presence.

In the area of Scotland where I grew up there are castles
scattered hither and yon across the landscape.
All around them lies the easy land, the fertile soil,
the soft and gentle woodlands, pastures, meadows.
But the castles tower high above, set firm on solid rock.
Volcanic plugs, they call these rocks: the solid,
basalt, lava core of old volcanoes, long extinct.
This is rock of such a solid, adamant hardness that weather,
storms and ice, can never touch it. It has survived
the glaciers of the Ice Age.

These castles are not, by any stretch of the imagination,
places of luxurious ease, convenience. Yet they too
have endured long after the easier, more convenient dwellings
all have crumbled into dust. They have been places, too,
of character: of heroism, honor, and high adventure.
And they all possess a magnetism, a lure of life and history,
legend, folklore, and song, which draws people still today
within their wide and circling walls to gaze
upon the ancient rock and wonder.

Saint Paul wrote, in Corinthians, "The Rock was Christ."
Might I, Lord, take the wondrous qualities
of those ancient fortresses—their endurance,
their magnetism, their security, their power to inspire—
and claim it for my life in you? That is what you ask,
invite, urge me to do this night. That is the call,
the offer, and the challenge of your Sermon on the Mount.

Then let me build my life on you—on Christ
the solid Rock—and live it here and now
for all eternity.
                    Amen.

DAY THIRTY-NINE
Authority
Matthew 7:28–29

And when Jesus finished these sayings, the crowds were astonished at his teaching, for he taught them as one who had authority, and not as their scribes.

MORNING

Various feelings have been mine, Lord, after listening
to a sermon. I have known interest, amusement, fascination,
anger, and frustration. I have felt troubled,
conscience-burdened, even sometimes bored.
But I have never felt astonished.

Astonishment is a rare emotion in a world where
the most incredible and unthinkable things seem to happen
every other day. Even in the movies, on TV, one can see
such a host of elaborate special effects—spaceships,
monsters, earthquakes, and such—that what might,
fifty years ago, have appeared well-nigh miraculous
is, today, another routine piece of technological showmanship.
Yes, Lord, it's hard to be astonished anymore.

I wonder what it was about you, and your teaching,
that so astonished those who heard. Could it, perhaps,
have been your wisdom, your sagacity? After all,
folk don't expect profundity from a simple
country carpenter who never went to proper school,
certainly never could have read the ancient scholars,
sages, and philosophers. Yet you spoke such clear
and powerful truths that people gasped
and murmured to themselves, "That's right, you know!
That's something I have always thought was true, deep down,

but never have been able to hold on to,
let alone put into words."

Someone has written that you spoke
with "the authority of silence." Unlike the rest of us,
you spent long hours, days, even seasons alone with God,
treasuring, meditating, musing over the wisdom
of the Jewish people: wisdom that must have been passed down
by rabbis, I suppose, in the synagogue at Nazareth.
But you made that wisdom all your own, Lord,
simplified and reshaped it until it came forth
from your lips fresh forged, bright with the glow of heaven.

They were astonished also at your style;
not only what you said, but how you said it.
Over against the stale, flat, cistern water of the scribes,
with their endless debating of the jots and tittles
of the law, you brought the fresh, clear, cool,
and living water of a mountain spring,
bubbling up from unseen depths to cool the face and hands
and set the lips to song.

Astonish me now, Lord, by the sheer grandeur
of your Word, by the unearned gift of this new day;
by your call to me for service in the vineyard.
Let this astonishment show forth in joy
that will communicate to all I meet this day.
                                        Amen.

138

EVENING

Your sayings bore authority, Lord Christ,
and that authority astonished all who heard them.
They must have been dumbfounded at the claim you made:
not an explicit claim at this stage, but implicit beneath
everything you said in this Sermon on the Mount.

For example, when you said, "You have heard
that it was said of old, 'You shall not kill . . .'
But I say unto you, 'Do not be angry,' "
people knew that Moses was the source
that you were citing; rather, that Moses
brought this commandment straight from God.
Therefore to presume to correct or deepen such a hallowed word
could mean only one thing. The speaker must believe
that he is not just Moses' equal, but also God's.
No wonder that those crowds were so amazed!

The ultimate authority, however, for these teachings,
that which gave them such astonishing validity,
was your love: was the profound compassion, tenderness,
that showed itself in every moment of your ministry.
You spoke, not merely as a scholar interpreting the law,
not only as a prophet proclaiming holy righteousness,
but as the Son of God himself, come to show God's love,
to live it out right here in our midst.
Indeed, you not only showed the way, but you alone,
in love, could also offer help to walk that way.
Your words not only taught, they bore power
to assist their own fulfillment. They ministered
the strength of God, grace to begin anew, the secret
of true living through prayer, fellowship, and obedience.

And this authority of love, a love that triumphs
even over death—death which had seemed, till then,
the final grim authority—this authority of love,
you told us, is the authority of God.
Thus God, in love, through you, has conquered death
and all death's crushing power. And we are liberated,
once for all. Set free for life, for life in love forever.

Set your authority clear over me, Jesus my Lord,
over my hopes, my fears, my failures, my accomplishments.
And under this authority of love, let me rest
this night in peace.

Amen.

DAY FORTY
Continuing in Prayer
Proverbs 8:34

Blessed is the one that heareth me, watching daily at my gates, waiting at the posts of my doors.

MORNING

You have spoken much of prayer
in this great Sermon, Lord. Given me,
through these your words, at least a framework
upon which to raise a temple of my own, a sanctuary
where I might encounter you each day.

The foundation must be faith: trust that God,
through all the tragedy and triumph, the mystery
and miracle of life, is still, and above all else, my Father.
Faith that in God's will lies all
that is worth hoping for, worth living for.

The strong and sturdy walls of my own house
of prayer must be persistence, as you taught me, Lord.
That my prayers be not a sometime thing, an occasional pursuit
when I have urgent need for help or nothing better left to do.
May they rather form the shape and the structure
of my days; enclose the good, shut out the evil and
the cruel, lend grace and dignity and style
to all I undertake, seek to accomplish.

There will be rooms
within this temple, Lord, rooms for every mood
and moment of my praying. A Confessing Room,
where failure can be faced and dealt with,

then forgiven in your grace. A room for my petitions,
seeking guidance, strength, and courage for each day.
An Intercession Room—a large room, this—
where family, friends, yes, even enemies,
will all be welcomed, brought before the throne
of grace. And then, a central hall, bright-furnished
for thanksgiving, Lord, and praise: full of instruments
and song, resounding with joyful laughter.

The roof, of course, is love,
rainbow-arching over all in glory, lifting eyes
to gaze in wonder at its wide-branching pillars,
gaily colored panels, radiant lights; and beaming down
on everything below, your benediction
and your peace.

Assist me, Lord, in building
such a house of prayer. Then claim it
for your own. That in your house, forever more,
my dwelling place might be.
                              Amen.

EVENING

Forty days and forty nights, Lord Jesus,
a traditional, historical, liturgical, and mystical
portion of time. Forty days and nights that you have
spoken with me, chastened me, corrected, comforted, and
challenged me through this rich treasure house of prayer,
the Sermon on the Mount.

Forty days and nights in which,
like Moses and the people of the exodus
I have been on a journey, expedition, pilgrimage
toward a promised land that you have shown to me.
By day, the pillar of cloud, by night a tower of fire
to lift my eyes above the commonness of things,
the numbing routine chores, and catch the banners
on the hilltops, your emblems there
of victory and homecoming.
There have been times of doubt,
of faithlessness. The golden calves have
blinded me with all their tawdry, tinsel glitter.
The discipline of exodus, of campaigning through a wilderness,
has brought me to rebellion, to toying with the smooth idea
of turning back, reclaiming the old self-protective
chains that held me fast while I thought
I was free. Forgive me, Lord, my second thoughts,
my temporary strayings from the narrow way.

Forty days and nights, Lord,
like Elijah's fearful, panicked journey
fleeing from King Ahab for his life until
he found his life within the still small voice,
his mission and his purpose in his call from you
to return to where oppression, injustice, and idolatry
laid crushing yokes upon your people, Lord.

Forty days and forty nights, Lord Jesus,
like your testing in the desert, a testing that
took every ounce of strength, every inch of inner fortitude,
every particle of hope and faith and love in order
to come through. Yet you emerged the victor,
immeasurably strengthened for the way that lay ahead.

May this pilgrimage bear such results for me, Lord.
Let me learn from all its hazards and its falterings.
May I grow through every moment I have sensed
your holy presence. Let me live, from this time forward,
with a newer, fuller, richer, far, awareness of your grace,
my need, and all the hopes you place in me.

So bless my rest this night, and my arising.
Then send me forth again to be
"about my Father's business."

Amen.